Six Traits of Writing for English Language Learners

A guide to effective writing instruction for low-proficiency ELLs

by Holley Wilson Mayville

Table of Contents

Introduction

The Purpose of This Book

The Six Traits Model of writing assessment is an excellent tool to incorporate into writing instruction for English language learners (ELLs). The bulk of this volume is dedicated to ready-made activities that can start lower-proficiency English learners on the process of writing using the Traits. To help fit the Six Traits Model into your program, this book will give you an overview of the model, the advantages it presents for your ELL students, and the ways it can correlate to existing standards.

Why One School District Adopted the Six Traits Model:

After teaching English as a Second Language (ESL) in middle and high schools in Charlotte, North Carolina for 8 years, I was offered the position of ESL resource teacher for all of the high schools in the district. Stepping out of the trenches of the classroom and into Central Office, I realized that one of the great advantages of my new job would be the chance to look at what I had been teaching from a more global perspective: to analyze, compare and to have the time to read the research.

As I joined Central Office, the No Child Left Behind revolution was just revving up. In North Carolina, because we did not have a 10th grade English test, the 10th grade reading standard was evaluated rather unusually: in order to "pass" the standard, a student needed to perform at grade-level on both the 9th grade English test and the 10th grade writing assessment.

The ELL subgroup, which is rather sizeable in Charlotte, was performing abysmally. They struggled with the multiple-choice 9th grade English end-of-course test, which evaluates literary understanding and grammar. The few students who did pass that test, however, were sunk by the holistically graded writing test. In 2005, less than 10% of high school ELL students passed the 10th grade writing test, and there was a 40 point gap between their passing percentage and that of the non-ELL students. Adequate Yearly Progress (AYP) was not being made and ELL writing performance was a major factor: it was time to start learning how to teach writing.

I love to write, and I absolutely hated teaching writing to my students. I was trying to encourage critical thought and personal expression, but was constantly bogged down by the fact that none of my students seemed to be familiar with capitalization or the use of the period. So the writing would come to a screeching halt, and we'd go back to spelling drills, grammar drills, punctuation drills. Then I'd assign some more writing and be disappointed all over again. When I had a class of seniors who had to complete a state-mandated research paper, I wound up spending hours with each student and poring over their drafts, which were just a sea of purple marks (purple's less upsetting than red, you know). The entire experience was a misery for my students and for me. A quick poll of my fellow teachers around the district revealed that this sentiment was widely shared.

The Six Traits model allows you to look at the most (seemingly) disastrous of efforts, tease out the elements of writing present, and recognize the good things that are there and that can be built upon. This is perfect for ELL students, whose very identification is all about deficits, even thought they are as intelligent, creative, motivated and rich in experience as any other group of students. The Six Traits Model allows a teacher to define a student's writing not through its deficits, but through its progression. For students who are constantly facing their inadequacies in an alien world, such a constructive approach is essential.

What is the Six Traits Model? Why is it Appropriate for ELL Students?

The Six Traits Model finds its origins in the work of teachers who could not find a satisfactory assessment approach for writing, and who worked together, examining student products, looking for the essential elements of good writing. They went on to express their findings as a cohesive model: six traits of good writing. These traits are: Ideas, Organization, Voice, Word Choice, Sentence Fluency, and Conventions.

By identifying and labeling these traits, then defining the standards of quality within each trait, the teachers and researchers gave writing assessment and instruction a shared vocabulary and a simpler, more focused approach.

For students, the Six Traits Model allows them to concentrate on improving one trait at a time, with clear definitions and expectations for each trait. ELL students in particular can be utterly overwhelmed by the writing process, which is occurring in a new language and often in a new academic format from what they have been taught in their home countries. The trait-by-trait focus offered by the model is the perfect antidote to the deluge of challenges presented by a writing assignment. And, because Voice and Ideas are examined separately from Word Choice and Conventions, it is possible for students to discover areas of strength even in their earliest attempts, making writing the gratifying process it should be rather than the daunting process it often is.

For teachers, the two major challenges of teaching writing are explaining what is "good" in a subjective discipline and getting the papers graded. The unified vocabulary and standards of the Six Traits Model overcome the first challenge, and the narrowed focus of evaluating trait-by-trait help endlessly with the second. Teachers of ELL students will be as gratified as their charges to finally have a lens through which they may find positive attributes in student work, where before they were only seeing a wasteland of mechanical errors and limited vocabulary.

How Can the Six Traits Model be Correlated to Existing Standards?

In North Carolina, secondary ELL students are beholden to two sets of state-mandated standards for writing: the WiDA English proficiency standards and the standards used by the state to grade the 10th grade writing test.

WiDA is a research consortium that has created English language development standards and assessment tools now used by 23 states.

The WiDA writing standards are applied to three different aspects of student writing: linguistic complexity – which incorporates Sentence Fluency and Organization, vocabulary usage – which obviously addresses Word Choice, and language control – essentially Conventions. Ideas, Voice and Presentation are not really addressed directly in this rubric, but it is necessary to remember that these are language proficiency standards, not intelligence or style standards, and a basic premise that language proficiency researchers hold to is that a genius and a fool can both be equally proficient in a language.

2010 was the last year for implementation of the North Carolina state writing test for 10th graders. However, in the meantime, the advent of Common Core standards and the specter of Common Core-aligned standardized tests that reflect this document's emphasis on writing have ensured that writing is now more important than ever.

At first glance, the Common Core standards specifically labeled "Writing" would be overwhelming to a teacher of low-proficiency ELLs, especially those at the secondary level. The standards speak to the creation of complex academic texts and the elements of their development. However, the Common Core has two features that should be gratifying to the educators obligated to use it: as it steps forward through the grade-levels, it builds upon itself – elementary students and high school students alike are expected to write argumentative texts, but the components in those texts increase in complexity as the standards progress; and the final objective the Common Core is stepping toward is one of rigor and academic quality.

So, a low-proficiency ELL walks into a secondary classroom and it seems to the teacher that the administration, the standards and the state-mandated tests all expect this student to miraculously produce at an extremely advanced level. Of course, this is impossible, but it is still a worthy point on the horizon toward which we should aim our trajectories. The spiraling nature of the Common Core standards means that the teacher can refer to lower-grade standards for instruction and see clearly the path on which to build student performance toward grade-level proficiency.

Meanwhile, let's be frank: a student is never going to be able to "write informative/explanatory texts to examine and convey complex ideas, concepts, and information clearly and accurately through the effective selection, organization, and analysis of content" if they don't first simply start writing. And the very language of this standard (Common Core Writing Standard 2 for 11-12th graders) meshes neatly with the language of the Six Traits (ideas, organization, clearly and accurately). Use Six Traits from the very beginning and, in time, the students will be ready to achieve this lofty goal.

When looking at these two sets of standards for writing, it's clear that different agencies put emphasis on different elements. The Six Traits Model is comprehensive: it addresses all aspects of good writing. If one were to teach writing addressing all six traits, then prepare students for state assessments by identifying the traits stressed in those assessments, students would have all the tools at hand to be successful and would even have a little insight into how those tools will enhance their performance on a particular test.

How Can the Six Traits Model be Incorporated into an Existing Curriculum?

The key is to teach the students what the traits are and how the traits are evaluated. Once they understand that, then the Six Traits Model can become an integral part of any writing assignment – from short homework answers to term papers.

In Charlotte, secondary level ESL classes include students with proficiencies ranging from no English at all to WiDA's* fourth level of proficiency, Expanding,   While the traits can and should be part of the class culture from day one, the direct instruction of the traits described in this book will be most effective for students who have been in US schools for at least one year, and have attained the second level of proficiency, Emerging, or better.

The Six Traits Model needs to take on an everyday role in your classroom. The traits should be posted on the wall (there are posters available, or you and your students could make your own) as part of an ongoing reminder of their application to all writing tasks. Any paper or project rubrics should include the traits. They should be mentioned in conjunction with reading tasks (i.e. "Notice Faulkner's Word Choice here…") and grammar tasks (i.e. "By using subordinate clauses, we can expand our sentences and improve our Sentence Fluency…").

Direct instruction of the traits – what they are and what good execution looks like – is all about using good writing as a model. Know your students' reading proficiency, and use samples within and just beyond their ability to illustrate each trait. Have the students begin by identifying and describing the traits within example texts, then have them try their hand at the trait by writing in response to the text or by using the text as a model.

This book will provide self-contained writing activities that may be used on their own or as models for extension activities directly related to your curriculum. Because the book is intended as an introduction for ESL students, the traits come into the picture one by one, as students should be ready to learn about them, and are addressed individually with each writing task. More about introducing, teaching and evaluating each trait will be discussed as the traits emerge in the book.

* Because the WiDA proficiency standards are now used by 23 states and are easily located online at www.wida.us, I will be applying WiDA proficiency descriptors to students with whom certain strategies and activities might be used.

A model lesson will also be presented for each trait as it comes up in the book, to help demonstrate how the trait might be introduced. We'll begin with the first model lesson here, to help present the basic idea of traits and rubrics:

Model Lesson 1 – Assessing Writing With Traits

Content Objective: Students will be able to recognize that evaluating writing can be subjective. Students will be able to understand that a written piece has several different elements, or traits, that can be evaluated separately, and that the method for subjective evaluation is through the use of a rubric.

Language Objective: Students will be able to apply the terms subjective and objective to different forms of evaluation. Students will be able to describe how a piece of writing can be separated into traits and those traits evaluated for quality by using a rubric. Students will be able to identify and respond to the terms *trait, rubric, quality* and *assess*.

Connecting With Prior Knowledge/Building Background:

Before you begin, students must already understand that written responses are an important and ever-present element of their academic work.

Teacher Input/ Practice and Application:

Find two paintings of the same subject by different artists and in different styles – I would suggest a painting of a clown by Picasso and by Degas, both easily found on the Internet. Show them one painting.

Ask them, point-blank, "Is this picture good or bad?" If students are not immediately forthcoming with opinions, use "thumbs up/thumbs down" to poll them for their reactions. Ask both a supporter and a detractor for the reasons behind their response. The point of this discussion is to show that it's not easy to agree on whether a work of art is good or bad.

At this point, define "subjective" and "objective" by using the following examples:
subjective – "I think that I shall never see/ a poem lovely as a tree"
objective – $7,310 + 55 = 7,365$
Compare and contrast the two, and remind students that the difference is similar to that of "fact" and "opinion."

Return to the picture and comment that, yes, assessing it (and here define "assess," the simple phrase, "decide how good it is," can suffice) is not easy because it is subjective.

Now add the second painting to the mix and inform the students that their task will be to decide which one is better. Tell the students that the process will be easier if they take the pictures apart.

Move the students into groups of three or four, and ask each group to brainstorm together what the different parts of a picture could be. What we're looking for here are elemental things, such as "color" and "shapes" and "subject". Get the students started with one or two examples and then let them brainstorm on their own.

Pull the groups back together and put all the words they have brainstormed on the board. These words are the *traits* of the pictures. Decide on about five that can be used to compare and judge the pictures' quality.

Now we need to define quality. First, read *Zen and the Art of Motorcycle Maintenance* to establish that this can't actually be done, unless you're clinically insane, on a pointless road trip and off your meds. Then simplify this for the kids by explaining that *quality* is how good something is.

Make three columns on the board and label them thusly:

Not Good	Good	The Best

Take one of the traits, perhaps "color" and model thinking through how to define the quality of a pictures color, filling in the above. For example, it could read like this:

Not Good	Good	The Best
The colors are wrong or don't make sense. The artist picked ugly colors or colors that clash with each other.	Colors make sense in the picture. They don't clash with each other.	Colors are bright, they make sense in the picture and they make the picture more beautiful.

Ask each group to complete the columns in the same fashion for the other traits you have selected. You will definitely need to supervise this activity closely and guide the students toward:
- selecting good traits by which to judge the two paintings
- ensure that the quality of each trait is defined clearly and appropriately in each column

The students should complete this activity on overhead transparencies or on poster-sized paper that can be posted at the front of the room. Once the activity is completed and posted, inform the students that what they have just created is called a "rubric" and that the class will now use the rubric to judge the two paintings.

As a whole group, discuss each trait of the paintings and assign a "Not Good", "Good" or "The Best" score to each trait for each painting.

Review for Mastery:

Bring up two stories or poems that the class has studied recently. Hopefully there is a piece you can mention that the students either hated or loved. Ask the students how the activity you just completed with the two pictures can be used to decide which piece of writing is better. Depending on their proficiency, they can operate through oral discussion or they can write brief answers as a ticket out.

Section One
Before Sentences

For the Teacher...

Every teacher has squirreled away somewhere a piece of student work or two that stands out. My best student treasure is from a vocabulary assignment I gave my sixth grade ESL students years ago. In those days my classes were always very mixed in terms of English proficiency, so I tried to come up with assignments that allowed even the Newcomers some level of success, while all students were gaining something from the activity. This was easy when it came to vocabulary: ask students to illustrate the words.

I didn't know Jose was an artist – and it may be that he wasn't, but that he was still at the point where traditional symbolic conventions hadn't accreted in his mind, forcing him to draw stick figures in the middle of the page. The word he chose was "destruction," and the poster he drew featured a fiery car wreck practically leaping off the paper, a proto-cubist disregard for depth or composition giving a chaotic energy to the drawing that completed the assignment to a T. Jose hadn't been in the United States for a year, but he took this opportunity to show his understanding and he used it well.

How frustrating must it be to have a bright, inquisitive mind trapped behind the barrier of language? And asking ELL students to express themselves through writing when, on the face of things it seems that's the one thing they cannot do, feels almost cruel.

In the early years of my teaching ESL I didn't have the benefit of Lucy Calkins workshops and Sam Swope's memoir *I Am a Pencil* to inform my curriculum (let's be honest: I didn't have a curriculum). I made up how to teach English as I went along, trying to keep lessons creative, dynamic and challenging. I say jokingly sometimes that I kept the thinking-skills bar high in my classes so that *I* wouldn't die of boredom, but my kids, independent of their supposed proficiency, always rose to the challenge. I believe that's because the kids had something to say, and I asked them to say it in ways that overcame their language limitations. In this day and age one shouldn't have to remind anybody that "ELL" in no way equals "unintelligent," but I still struggle trying to convince teachers that the kids can handle the content. The kids want to think. It's finding a way to ask them to do it that addresses their English limitations which is hard.

It was gratifying to learn, once I came to Central Office and had time to read the research, that my initial ideas about lesson and assignment design were on track. Calkins points out in her series *Units of Study for Primary Writing* that writing begins in young children long before they can spell words or form sentences: it is the act of putting pencil to paper to express that is the seed of authorship. At the secondary level, diagrams, comics, movie posters, and illustrated vocabulary words, are all ways a student can discuss an idea on paper without having to rely on a full mastery of English.

The first section of this book is intended to get students started applying pencil to page, to explore and expand their expression in English, to help them develop their vocabulary in preparation for more extensive assignments, and to help them begin to understand the Six Traits assessment process.

Three traits will be assessed on these prompts: Ideas, Word Choice, and Presentation. The goal for basic mastery at this point is for students to understand their prompt and perform the tasks in English successfully. To exceed expectations at this point, we will look for students to show creativity in their responses to these fairly simple prompts, and for them to push the boundaries of what their skills in English will allow them to express.

The trait rubric applicable to each entry appears at the bottom of each entry page. You will need to circle the descriptor that best characterizes the student's performance with that trait on that task. There is space also for comments. The rubrics on the assignment pages are written in teacher-friendly language, rather than student-friendly language, so you should take advantage of the comment space provided, as well as a brief oral conference with the student, to express the strengths and weaknesses you detected in their response.

A student-friendly table of trait descriptors applicable to Section One appears on the page before the entries. Refer students to that page and discuss what the expectations are for their responses when beginning this section, and when necessary in assigning entries.

Trait: Ideas

Ideas are the content of the piece. To my mind, this trait is the most critical to effective writing, illustrated by the fact that a student who routinely cranks out mediocre writing will surprise you with a stunning piece *if he cares about what he has to say*. And the student cares about the content of the piece when it is a quality idea.

The trait of Ideas is a good place to start with ELLs , as quality ideas are not dependent on language for their existence. Even so, a "quality idea" is an ephemeral thing, and ELLs struggle as much as any other student to find them, and then can be hindered by their ability to comprehend what sort of ideas are being elicited from them and how to express the ideas once they've found them.

When teaching ELLs about Ideas, there are multiple elements you will want them to grasp:
- understand what the prompts or assignment is asking for
- select (from a possible multiplicity of responses) the best idea
- narrow the idea so that the response can address it fully
- elaborate on the idea
- discover the best details to convey the idea

The following sample lesson demonstrates how this trait might be introduced. Keep in mind that all sample lessons in this book are designed assuming that the previous sample lessons have been delivered (such as Sample Lesson 1 in the main introduction) and can be relied on as background knowledge.

Sample Lesson 2: Introducing the Trait of Ideas

Content Objective: Students will be able to define the trait of Ideas and identify features of that trait in a piece of writing. Students will be able to use a rubric to evaluate the quality of Ideas in a writing sample. Students will be able to discuss the quality of the trait of Ideas in their own writing.

Language Objective: Students will be able to identify and list features of the trait Ideas and use a rubric to assess a score on the trait for a writing sample.

Connecting with the Objectives:
Think-Pair-Share – students will read the objectives and consider the following two questions: What do you think we will do today?
                         What are three words we need to learn about today?
They will discuss their answers with a partner, and then each pair will share their best ideas with the class. Get a consensus on the important words to learn about and write those on the board by the objectives.

Connecting With Prior Knowledge/Building Background:
      What is a trait of good writing?
      How will we use traits to help our writing improve?

Teacher Input:
Provide students with two paragraphs on the same general topic, one of which is clearly boring and one of which is interesting and engaging. For example, you could use:

My Summer Vacation
by Qing-Jao

I did not go to school. I watched my little brother. He liked to fight with me. I watched TV. I called my friends on the phone. It was boring. It was fun sometimes, too, like when we went to story time at the library.

A Summer Day
by Carla

The sun was hot. The water was cold. I stood in the water. My legs were cold and my back was hot. The ocean was loud but I like the sound. I could go to the beach every day. I wish it was still summer vacation.

Ask students to read both then discuss:
      Which one do you like better?
      How are these paragraphs different?
      Why is this one better/worse?

Create a t-chart on the board with a column for "good" and a column for "bad". Ask students to give describing words that fit the good paragraph and the bad paragraph and record on the board. You're looking for things like "boring," "doesn't say anything," "funny," "interesting," to start with.

Give students a copy of the Ideas rubric, discuss how each paragraph fits into the rubric. Compare the t-chart on the board with the rubric and make notes on the board to link student statements with elements of the rubric.

Have students complete this stem sentence:
  "If my writing has good Ideas, then it will be _____."
  "If I am going to think of good Ideas for my writing, I need to
_____."
Students complete the sentences on their own, then move into groups of three or four. They need to discuss their individual answers and create a group answer for each stem, which they will then write out on a sentence strip to be posted in the Ideas area of your room.

Practice Activity:
Students need to complete a brief paragraph on the following prompt: think of a thing that everyone sees every day that is like yourself. What is the thing, and how is it similar to you?

I'm a puzzle, because I don't say much and I'm hard to figure out.

I'm a desk, as neat as can be…

I am a pencil, ready to write my life.

(from *I am a Pencil* by Sam Swope, pp 110-114).

Starter stems:
"I am a _____. I _____." or "I am a
_____, because _____."

Their choice needs to be both interesting and honest. Remind them that there is a difference between "I am a boy. I have hair." and "I am a pencil, ready to write my life." Also, as these paragraphs will be subjects of our first trait assessment, ask students to NOT include their names on the paper.

After pieces are finished (10 to 15 minutes), take up all papers, move students back into groups of four, and re-distribute the papers randomly and anonymously. Have groups assess each paper using the rubric, and then ask them to rank each paper. They will share the best paper they received and their explanation for why they decided it was the best, using language from the rubric.

Review for Mastery:

Ask students to define the important words recorded on the board from Connecting with Objectives.

Success Descriptors

Not Yet	Emerging	Effective	Strong
Pictures/Words do not address prompt. Ideas, if any, do not relate to prompt.	Pictures/Words attempt to respond to prompt. Ideas are inaccurate.	Pictures/Words respond to prompt. Ideas are simple and show clear understanding.	Pictures/Words go beyond a simple response to prompt. Ideas are original, fresh, and unique reflecting creative thought.

Just because an ELL is not yet at all proficient in English does not mean that their head is not full of great ideas and a thorough understanding of the world around them. Their challenge is to express those great ideas despite the limitations of their English proficiency. When evaluating for Ideas, try to look past the simplicity, or perhaps even crudeness of the expression to the accuracy and originality of the approach the student has taken to his or her response.

Trait: Word Choice

As a painter selects colors for her palette, scrutinizing each hue and tint to decide if it is the one that will capture the light just so, so does a writer select words. The English language, if nothing else, must be celebrated for the vast collection of words, drawn from an array of cultures and eras and seemingly endless in its range of shades of meaning.

However, an ELL is often still stuck with the basic starter paint kit, faced with equaling Tintoretto while only having access to the primary colors.

Vocabulary is a massive deficit for ELLs, and a constant game of catch-up, especially at the secondary level. Students acquire common, everyday words first, then move towards more specific, technical and academic terms as they progress.

For native speakers of English, the Word Choice trait is intended to assess the accuracy and elegance of word selection, to move toward refinement: are they "conjoined" or "attached"? Should one "ascend" or "arise"? Was he "deposed" or "overthrown"? For ELLs, however, the assessor first must ask, is the word correct? As the ELL's vocabulary grows, and there are more words to choose from, clarity of meaning and appropriateness of register become more significant.

The best way to amass vocabulary is to read, and the best way to master that vocabulary is to use it in writing. Think about how the process works for you: let's pretend that you've never encountered the word "accrete" before in your readings, yet you came across it earlier in this chapter ("I didn't know Jose was an artist – and it may be that he wasn't, but that he was still at the point where traditional symbolic conventions hadn't accreted in his mind, forcing him to draw stick figures in the middle of the page.") "Accrete" sounds like the more familiar "concrete" and "accrue," and those associations, along with the overall context, could bring to mind an image of boring symbolic conventions hardening in barnacle-like layers on the walls of a growing young mind (at least, I hope it worked that way: it's what I was going for). And a quick check of dictionary.com will confirm that "accrete" means "to add, as by growth." But you don't need to check dictionary.com, because just by grasping the image of the sentence, you've understood "accrete," and at some later date you'll be hunting for a word that conveys a similar image, and "accrete" will pop up, and you'll try it and it will sound good, and you'll move on, a confident master of yet another English word.

That's really how it works, and this natural path of acquisition should be part of the process as the ESL teacher is guiding and accelerating vocabulary growth for ELLs. The students encounter the words in reading, understand the words through a choice of strategies (to be discussed momentarily), then gain confidence with the words by attempting to use them in writing.

Teach the students the strategies we use to determine the meanings of words: gleaning from context or examining the word's relationship with more familiar words with similar roots or prefixes. Guide understanding by providing known synonyms or using the word in demonstrative examples ("He pulled the *skean dhu* out from under his kilt and stabbed the man repeatedly." A *skean dhu* is a… A. musical instrument from China, B. fish from Algeria, or C. dagger from Scotland.) which allow the student to make the connections and come to the understanding with his or her own thinking.

Note how I do not mention the dictionary as a teaching tool. It is a tool, and a useful one, but not for initial instruction of vocabulary. After finishing this chapter, you may well remember what *accrete* and *skean dhu* mean, but will you remember that a *panavane* is a "knife-bearing torpedo-like device for cutting mines adrift"? It's less likely.

Beyond that, a well-meaning second-language learner with a bilingual dictionary can be a dangerous thing indeed: I cite my own French short story, *"Jorgll, L'herisson Brave"* – which I thought was about a stalwart hedgehog, but turned out to refer to a "nice, but stupid porcupine" – as a cautionary tale. Or the fellow tasked with translating a promotional brochure for the seaside resort of La Grande Motte (The Great Dune), who selected from his French-English dictionary the far more appealing "The Big Lump," earning points for accuracy but not, perhaps, for elegance.

Encourage your students to make their initial attempts without any dictionary at all. This is a good time to reinforce the concept of the rough draft. Let the students use words that work as placeholders, then show them how to go back and analyze them within the complete draft. Are they repetitive or overused? Can a dictionary or thesaurus provide a choice that works better?

The model lesson below shows how the Trait of Word Choice can be introduced.

Model Lesson 3 – Introducing Word Choice

Content Objective: Students will be able to recognize the importance of accuracy and specificity in word choice in writing.

Language Objective: Students will be able to compare and contrast "general" words versus "specific" words. Students will be able to alter their vocabulary choices in a particular task from the general to the specific.

Connecting With Objectives/Connecting With Prior Knowledge/Building Background:
What trait of writing has the class already learned about (Ideas)?
Who can guess, of the six remaining traits and using the objectives, which trait will be studied next?
Why might choosing words well help with writing? (there is the obvious explanation that writing is constructed entirely out of words. See what else your students think of)

Teacher Input

Write the word HOUSE on the board. Tell the students that they each have 10 to 15 minutes to draw a house… but there are some rules:
- it must be a house they have seen in real life
- they can't look at their neighbor's drawings or let anyone look at theirs – the goal is to be completely original
- so try to think of a house that they have seen in real life that no one else would think of drawing
- they need to include as many details about the house (not the people, not the plants around it, the house itself) as they can remember

When they are done, the students must take their drawing and a sheet of writing paper and have a "tea party." In this group exercise, they must move around the room, meet up with another student, compare pictures and then make note of the differences. Use a timer and allow students one minute for each meeting. After each minute is up, students must mill around and find a different partner to compare with.

After five turns of this, regroup as a whole class and have students call out the differences they wrote down. Hopefully, these will refer to the size and shape of the houses and the construction materials. Write down the words, organizing them into a word cloud – possibly like this:

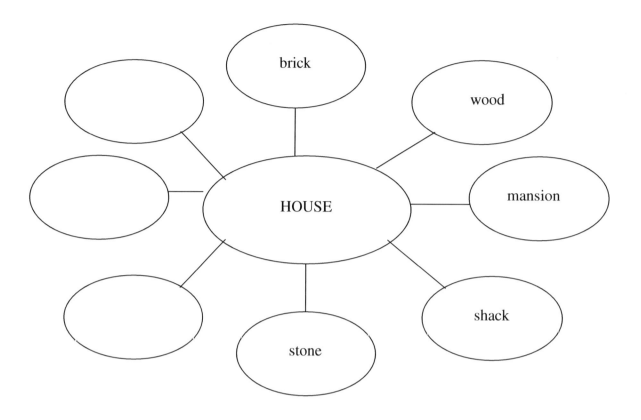

Discuss how the word "house" is a very useful word, but "three-story stone mansion" and "tiny log cabin" take the idea in two entirely different directions.

Now would be a good time to define the terms "general" and "specific" in this context. A general vocabulary word has the bonus of being easy to use and readily understood, but it doesn't tell you much, while a specific word, even though it is less-well known and requires some thought, can tell you much more in the same amount of time. Compare these two sentences:

The man went to the place.

Barack Obama went to the White House.

These are essentially the same sentence, but ask the students to think about how much more they know from the second sentence than from the first and why. At this point share the Word Choice rubric and talk about how each sentence would fit in the rubric.

The rubric puts some emphasis on words "relating to the prompt" and being "accurate." Discuss why these are important. If necessary give an example: using a drawing from the house assignment, remind students that they were asked to talk to each other about how the houses in the pictures were different. Pretend you are a student doing that task and say, "the two flowers are friends" or "my dog has white fur". Ask the students to tell you why these two statements are not helpful. Ask them for a statement that is accurate and relates to the prompt (is correct and answers the question).

Practice/Application:
Now, ask them to look at the following two pictures:

This is the challenge: the students will secretly select one of the two pictures and write down what they see. When they are done, they will get in teams of three or four (whatever grouping you can attain in equal sizes) and exchange papers. Each team will earn a point for correctly guessing which picture was described.

Remind the students that, in order to help their teammates pick the right description, they will have to be specific in their details, as the two pictures, in the general sense, are remarkably alike.

Get back into a whole group and have students volunteer up a paper they think is a good response and one that was not so good (i.e. nobody could guess which picture it was talking about). Use the Word Choice rubric to discuss the qualities of each response.

Review for Mastery:

In this chapter, the limited vocabulary of beginning ELLs is acknowledged as the activities center around building through association and exploration. As the descriptors below indicate, broad accuracy and creativity are the main points of focus at this early stage.

Success Descriptors

Not Yet	Emerging	Effective	Strong
No English words are used. Word choices do not relate to prompt.	English words relate to prompt. Word choice is weak and at times inaccurate.	English words address prompt. Word choice is simplistic and basic.	English words respond to prompt. Word choice includes synonyms and words that are more complex.

The most important thing a low-proficiency ELL can be doing at this point is collecting and using English words. For your part, please encourage risk-taking and experimentation. The fastest English learners are the ones who will bravely use a new word, even if they aren't entirely confident of it's meaning – and you don't want to discourage such bravery. A student who shows mastery at this point is one who uses vocabulary with which they are familiar (probably because you have taught it to them) in an appropriate fashion. A student who excels at this point is one who dares to try new words, with some degree of success in expressing their idea.

Chapter 1 Activities

The assignments in this section follow four basic formats that should not be too intimidating for your students, and which will elicit successful responses for students at the Emerging level of proficiency.

The first format is a labeled picture. The prompts will ask students to "Draw a…." then "Write about …" You will need to model responding to this type of response. In order not to "inspire" copycat responses, address your model to this prompt:
Draw your desk. Write about your desk.

You will need to draw your own desk on the board (or on poster-board, so you can leave it up for future reference). Be sure to include real details, such as your coffee mug, the messy pile of un-graded papers, or the fantasy novel you have hidden under your grammar textbook. Then label the picture with the names of the items you have included in your drawing, using vocabulary that you would have already taught the class in an "Elements of the Classroom" vocabulary unit, found in every newcomer ESL textbook in the known universe. Use a labeling system, such as writing above the object named, or connecting the word to the object with and arrow.

The second format is the "word cloud," which is a precursor to the graphic organizer known as "spider maps." The prompt will be a picture of an object, surrounded by ovals connected to the object with lines. The expectation is that the student will fill in the ovals with words associated with the picture. These words can be descriptive, can express actions that the object might perform, can categorize the object, or can represent sub-categories of the object. The sky's the limit, as long as the connection between the word and the object is clear. Again, you will need to model, and again we'll provide you with a separate prompt for modeling:

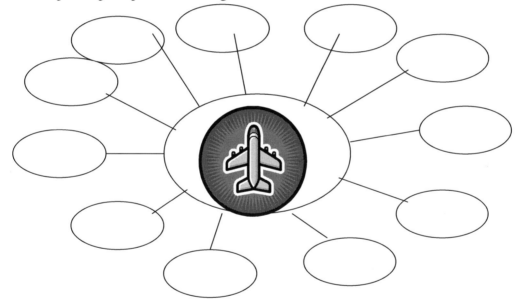

Eleven bubbles to fill – that's pretty evil, but it will push the students to get creative. Obviously you've got such words as "airplane," "plane," "fly," and "wings." Once you've addressed those basics, try more obscure approaches, and model using your dictionary – "metal," "tail," "pilot," "travel," "airport," "big," or "crash" – remember, you can describe, categorize, sub-categorize, or associate to come up with words.

The third style of prompts will be good, old-fashioned fill-in-the-blanks. The topics of these prompts should include concepts and vocabulary addressed in a newcomer's ESL textbook. Instead of modeling a separate prompt, teach the students how to do these by working as a group to complete the first prompt, selecting one student in the class (or yourself) as the subject. When evaluating these, focus on how well the student's choice of word or phrase completes the sentence and addresses the main topic in terms of content (not grammar).

The fourth and final style of prompt in this section is the Advertisement/Flier. Here students will be asked to use words and pictures to create advertisements for familiar products or fliers for familiar events. Instead of modeling, this time use real advertisements and fliers to show how they are done, the language used, and what could be included in the student responses. You will need to find: a used-car flier, a job advertisement from the classifieds, a clothing advertisement in a clothing catalogue, a restaurant or club opening flier, and a party invitation.

Student Friendly Rubric: Section One

TRAIT	Not Yet	Emerging	Effective	Strong
Ideas	You didn't answer the question. Your answer was not about the question.	You tried to answer the question, but you could have said more.	Answer the question – write about what you were told to write about. Write as many things as you can.	Answer the question with new, interesting ideas that no one else thought of. Tell more than the prompt asks you to tell.
Word Choice	You did not use English words. The English words you did use were not the right words and did not say what you wanted to say.	Some of the words you used were not the best English words to say what you wanted to say.	Use English words that you have learned. Check your dictionary for words you don't know. Use word you know correctly.	Use new words that you haven't studied yet and use them correctly – try your dictionary! See what works!

Entry 1
A New Friend
Talk to a person in your class. Draw that person. Write about that person.

Trait Assessment
Trait: Ideas
Success Descriptors (Circle one and add your own comments)

Not Yet	Emerging	Effective	Strong
Does not answer prompt or it is not possible to understand how response relates to prompt.	Picture and/or words answer prompt, but are simplest answer possible, very vague, or not very accurate.	Pictures and/or words answer prompt. Are simple but show clear understanding.	Prompt is answered, but ideas in product go beyond simple answer and show further creative thought.
Comments: _____ _____ _____	Comments: _____ _____ _____	Comments: _____ _____ _____	Comments: _____ _____ _____

Entry 2
My Home
Draw your home. Write about your home.

Trait Assessment
Trait: Word Choice
Success Descriptors (Circle one and add your own comments)

Not Yet	Emerging	Effective	Strong
Does not answer prompt. Makes no attempt to use English words.	Words are related to prompt, but are inaccurate choices.	Words answer prompt, but are basic choices.	Words answer prompt, an attempt at using multiple synonyms, more complex words has been made.
Comments: _____ _____ _____	Comments: _____ _____ _____	Comments: _____ _____ _____	Comments: _____ _____ _____

Entry 3

My Favorite Teacher
Draw a picture of your favorite teacher. Write about your favorite teacher.

Trait Assessment
Trait: Ideas
Success Descriptors (Circle one and add your own comments)

Not Yet	Emerging	Effective	Strong
Does not answer prompt or it is not possible to understand how response relates to prompt.	Picture and/or words answer prompt, but are simplest answer possible, very vague, or not very accurate.	Pictures and/or words answer prompt. Are simple but show clear understanding.	Prompt is answered, but ideas in product go beyond simple answer and show further creative thought.
Comments: _____ _____ _____	Comments: _____ _____ _____	Comments: _____ _____ _____	Comments: _____ _____ _____

Entry 4
The Classroom
Draw your classroom. Write about your classroom.

Trait Assessment
Trait: Word Choice
Success Descriptors (Circle one and add your own comments)

Not Yet	Emerging	Effective	Strong
Does not answer prompt. Makes no attempt to use English words.	Words are related to prompt, but are inaccurate choices.	Words answer prompt, but are basic choices.	Words answer prompt, an attempt at using multiple synonyms, more complex words has been made.
Comments: _____ _____ _____	Comments: _____ _____ _____	Comments: _____ _____ _____	Comments: _____ _____ _____

Entry 5
My Family
Draw your family. Write about your family.

___

Trait Assessment
Trait: Ideas
Success Descriptors (Circle one and add your own comments)

Not Yet	Emerging	Effective	Strong
Does not answer prompt or it is not possible to understand how response relates to prompt.	Picture and/or words answer prompt, but are simplest answer possible, very vague, or not very accurate.	Pictures and/or words answer prompt. Are simple but show clear understanding.	Prompt is answered, but ideas in product go beyond simple answer and show further creative thought.
Comments: _____ _____ _____	Comments: _____ _____ _____	Comments: _____ _____ _____	Comments: _____ _____ _____

Entry 6

Bus: Write words about a bus in each oval.

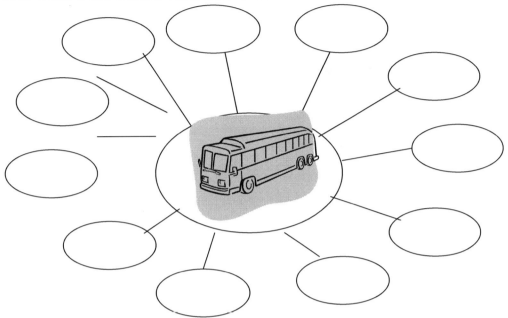

Trait Assessment
Trait: Word Choice
Success Descriptors (Circle one and add your own comments)

Not Yet	Emerging	Effective	Strong
Does not answer prompt. Makes no attempt to use English words.	Words are related to prompt, but are inaccurate choices.	Words answer prompt, but are basic choices.	Words answer prompt, an attempt at using multiple synonyms, more complex words has been made.
Comments: _____ _____	Comments: _____ _____	Comments: _____ _____	Comments: _____ _____

Entry 7
Shoe: Write words about shoes in each oval.

Trait Assessment
Trait: Ideas
Success Descriptors (Circle one and add your own comments)

Not Yet	Emerging	Effective	Strong
Does not answer prompt or it is not possible to understand how response relates to prompt.

Comments: _____
_____
_____ | Picture and/or words answer prompt, but are simplest answer possible, very vague, or not very accurate.

Comments: _____
_____
_____ | Pictures and/or words answer prompt. Are simple but show clear understanding.

Comments: _____
_____
_____ | Prompt is answered, but ideas in product go beyond simple answer and show further creative thought.

Comments: _____
_____
_____ |

Entry 8
Computer: Write words about computers in each oval.

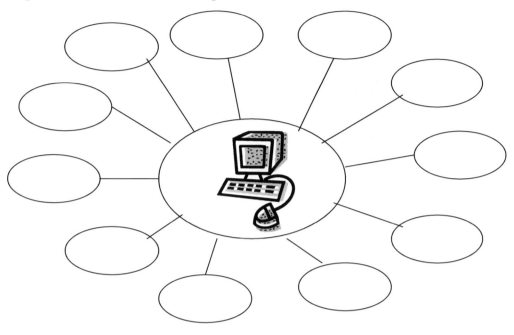

Trait Assessment
Trait: Word Choice
Success Descriptors (Circle one and add your own comments)

Not Yet	Emerging	Effective	Strong
Does not answer prompt. Makes no attempt to use English words.	Words are related to prompt, but are inaccurate choices.	Words answer prompt, but are basic choices.	Words answer prompt, an attempt at using multiple synonyms, more complex words has been made.
Comments: _____ _____ _____	Comments: _____ _____ _____	Comments: _____ _____ _____	Comments: _____ _____ _____

Entry 9
Book: Write words about books in each oval.

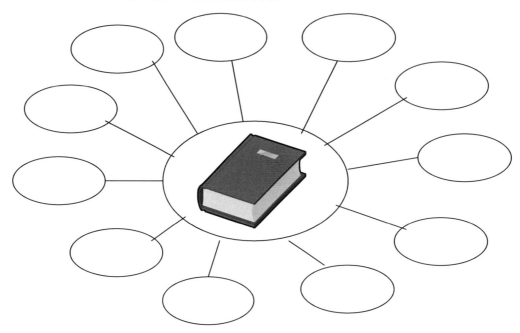

Trait Assessment
Trait: Ideas
Success Descriptors (Circle one and add your own comments)

Not Yet	Emerging	Effective	Strong
Does not answer prompt or it is not possible to understand how response relates to prompt.	Picture and/or words answer prompt, but are simplest answer possible, very vague, or not very accurate.	Pictures and/or words answer prompt. Are simple but show clear understanding.	Prompt is answered, but ideas in product go beyond simple answer and show further creative thought.
Comments: _____ _____ _____	Comments: _____ _____ _____	Comments: _____ _____ _____	Comments: _____ _____ _____

Entry 10
Cow: Write words about cows in each oval.

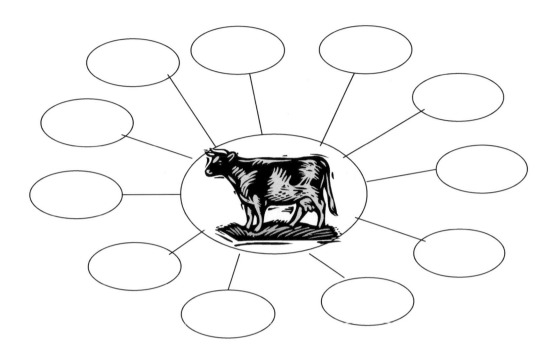

Trait Assessment
Trait: Word Choice
Success Descriptors (Circle one and add your own comments)

Not Yet	Emerging	Effective	Strong
Does not answer prompt. Makes no attempt to use English words.	Words are related to prompt, but are inaccurate choices.	Words answer prompt, but are basic choices.	Words answer prompt, an attempt at using multiple synonyms, more complex words has been made.
Comments: _____ _____ _____	Comments: _____ _____ _____	Comments: _____ _____ _____	Comments: _____ _____ _____

Entry 11
About Me: Write words in the blanks to make this paragraph about you.

My name is _____.

I am _____ years old.

I come from _____.

Now I live in _____.

I go to _____ school.

My _____'s name is _____.

Trait Assessment
Trait: Word Choice
Success Descriptors (Circle one and add your own comments)

Not Yet	Emerging	Effective	Strong
Does not answer prompt. Makes no attempt to use English words.	Words are related to prompt, but are inaccurate choices.	Words answer prompt, but are basic choices.	Words answer prompt, an attempt at using multiple synonyms, more complex words has been made.
Comments: _____ _____ _____	Comments: _____ _____ _____	Comments: _____ _____ _____	Comments: _____ _____ _____

Entry 12
Schedule: Write words in the blanks that tell about your class schedule.

My first class is _____.

My _____ class is _____.

My third _____ is _____.

My fourth class _____   _____.

I like my _____ class best.

I learn about _____ there.

Trait Assessment
Trait: Word Choice
Success Descriptors (Circle one and add your own comments)

Not Yet	Emerging	Effective	Strong
Does not answer prompt. Makes no attempt to use English words.	Words are related to prompt, but are inaccurate choices.	Words answer prompt, but are basic choices.	Words answer prompt, an attempt at using multiple synonyms, more complex words has been made.
Comments: _____ _____ _____	Comments: _____ _____ _____	Comments: _____ _____ _____	Comments: _____ _____ _____

Entry 13
Pets: Write words in the blanks to help explain about pets.

Pets are _____.

A _____ is one type of pet.

Another type of pet is a _____.

You can _____ with your pet.

It is important to always _____ your pet.

When you buy a pet, you should also buy _____,

_____, and _____.

Trait Assessment
Trait: Ideas
Success Descriptors (Circle one and add your own comments)

Not Yet	Emerging	Effective	Strong
Does not answer prompt or it is not possible to understand how response relates to prompt.	Picture and/or words answer prompt, but are simplest answer possible, very vague, or not very accurate.	Pictures and/or words answer prompt. Are simple but show clear understanding.	Prompt is answered, but ideas in product go beyond simple answer and show further creative thought.
Comments: _____ _____ _____	Comments: _____ _____ _____	Comments: _____ _____ _____	Comments: _____ _____ _____

Entry 14
The Store: Write words in the blanks that help tell about your trip to the store.

Sometimes I go to the store.

The store I go to is called _____.

I go there when I need _____.

You can also buy _____, _____,

and _____ at this store.

When I buy things at the store, I pay with _____.

I wish my store had _____.

Trait Assessment
Trait: Word Choice
Success Descriptors (Circle one and add your own comments)

Not Yet	Emerging	Effective	Strong
Does not answer prompt. Makes no attempt to use English words.	Words are related to prompt, but are inaccurate choices.	Words answer prompt, but are basic choices.	Words answer prompt, an attempt at using multiple synonyms, more complex words has been made.
Comments: _____ _____ _____	Comments: _____ _____ _____	Comments: _____ _____ _____	Comments: _____ _____ _____

Entry 15
My Home Country: Write words in the blanks to help tell about your home country.

I come from a country called _____.

It is near _____.

It has many _____.

People in my country _____.

I like my home country because it has _____

and _____.

I wish my country had _____.

Trait Assessment
Trait: Ideas
Success Descriptors (Circle one and add your own comments)

Not Yet	Emerging	Effective	Strong
Does not answer prompt or it is not possible to understand how response relates to prompt.	Picture and/or words answer prompt, but are simplest answer possible, very vague, or not very accurate.	Pictures and/or words answer prompt. Are simple but show clear understanding.	Prompt is answered, but ideas in product go beyond simple answer and show further creative thought.
Comments: _____ _____ _____	Comments: _____ _____ _____	Comments: _____ _____ _____	Comments: _____ _____ _____

Entry 16
Car Flier
You want to sell your car. Create a flier that tells people about your car. Draw a picture of your car. Write about the car. Tell people how much money your want for the car.

Trait Assessment
Trait: Ideas
Success Descriptors (Circle one and add your own comments)

Not Yet	Emerging	Effective	Strong
Does not answer prompt or it is not possible to understand how response relates to prompt.	Picture and/or words answer prompt, but are simplest answer possible, very vague, or not very accurate.	Pictures and/or words answer prompt. Are simple but show clear understanding.	Prompt is answered, but ideas in product go beyond simple answer and show further creative thought.
Comments: _____ _____ _____	Comments: _____ _____ _____	Comments: _____ _____ _____	Comments: _____ _____ _____

Entry 17
Job Advertisement
You are a boss and you need to hire someone to do a job. Write an advertisement to tell people about the job. Write about what kind of work the person would do, what kind of education* or experience** the person should have, and what you will pay the person to do the job.

Trait Assessment
Trait: Ideas
Success Descriptors (Circle one and add your own comments)

Not Yet	Emerging	Effective	Strong
Does not answer prompt or it is not possible to understand how response relates to prompt.	Picture and/or words answer prompt, but are simplest answer possible, very vague, or not very accurate.	Pictures and/or words answer prompt. Are simple but show clear understanding.	Prompt is answered, but ideas in product go beyond simple answer and show further creative thought.
Comments: _____ _____ _____	Comments: _____ _____ _____	Comments: _____ _____ _____	Comments: _____ _____ _____

* education: *how much school (high school, university, training) a person has had.*
** experience: *what kind of jobs a person has had*

Entry 18
Clothes Advertisement
You are a fashion designer*. Draw a wonderful outfit** that you would like to make and sell. Write about the outfit. Tell people why the outfit is cool. Tell people how much money each piece of the outfit will cost.

Trait Assessment
Trait: Word Choice
Success Descriptors (Circle one and add your own comments)

Not Yet	Emerging	Effective	Strong
Does not answer prompt. Makes no attempt to use English words.	Words are related to prompt, but are inaccurate choices.	Words answer prompt, but are basic choices.	Words answer prompt, an attempt at using multiple synonyms, more complex words has been made.
Comments: _____ _____ _____	Comments: _____ _____ _____	Comments: _____ _____ _____	Comments: _____ _____ _____

* Fashion designer: *a person who makes clothes.*
**outfit: *a set of clothes (jacket, pants, shirt, or skirt and blouse, for example) that look good together*

Entry 19
Restaurant Opening*
You are opening a new restaurant, and you want people to come and eat your food. Create a flier for your restaurant opening. Tell people when the opening is, where your restaurant is, and what kind of food your restaurant will have. You could draw a picture of your restaurant or your food, to help your flier look good.

Trait Assessment
Trait: Ideas
Success Descriptors (Circle one and add your own comments)

Not Yet	Emerging	Effective	Strong
Does not answer prompt or it is not possible to understand how response relates to prompt.

Comments: _____
_____
_____ | Picture and/or words answer prompt, but are simplest answer possible, very vague, or not very accurate.

Comments: _____
_____
_____ | Pictures and/or words answer prompt. Are simple but show clear understanding.

Comments: _____
_____
_____ | Prompt is answered, but ideas in product go beyond simple answer and show further creative thought.

Comments: _____
_____
_____ |

* restaurant opening: *the first day a restaurant is open. The can be a party or special prices for the food.*

Entry 20
Party Invitation
You are going to have a party. Create an invitation to tell your friends about the party. Write about when the party is, where the party is, and what event (a birthday? a holiday?) the party is for. Draw pictures on your invitation that show what kind of party it is and to make your invitation look good.

Trait Assessment
Trait: Word Choice
Success Descriptors (Circle one and add your own comments)

Not Yet	Emerging	Effective	Strong
Does not answer prompt. Makes no attempt to use English words.	Words are related to prompt, but are inaccurate choices.	Words answer prompt, but are basic choices.	Words answer prompt, an attempt at using multiple synonyms, more complex words has been made.
Comments: _____ _____ _____	Comments: _____ _____ _____	Comments: _____ _____ _____	Comments: _____ _____ _____

Section Two:
Simple Sentences

To the teacher....

The expectation in this section is that students will begin to respond using simple sentences. Before they begin work in this section, they should have received direct instruction in writing complete sentences (subject-verb, subject-verb-object, at a minimum) and in the conventions of using initial capitalization and ending punctuation.

Entries will be evaluated for Ideas and Word Choice again, as well as for Organization and Conventions. Let's examine the rubrics associated with the two new Traits.

Trait: Organization

In the 2000 film *Memento*, the main character suffers from long-term memory loss, yet wants to find the man who killed his wife. The audience, confined to the protagonist's impaired perceptions and understanding, must watch the story unfold backwards in order to solve the mystery. What earned *Memento* notice from the movie critics was not its story (Ideas) or cinematography (Voice) but its Organization. The structure of the film was driven by the fact of the hero's disability and in turn, a pedestrian mystery was elevated by its unique storytelling design.

It's not enough to have good ideas and to present them with an elegant turn of phrase. The order in which the ideas are delivered is crucial to the understanding of the overall theme. It is possible to structure a poem, story or essay in any umber of ways, at many levels of complexity. What makes for quality organization is the selection of a structure that best communicates the ideas.

At this point, your students may be limited in the extent or the complexity of their sentences and vocabulary, but they need not be limited in the area of organization, as it is not tied directly to the language itself. This gives you an opportunity to push students to use higher-order thinking and creativity, even as they are still operating with a lower English proficiency.

You probably already do discuss organization with your students, providing them with the conventional outlines of narrative (introduction, rising action, climax, denouement, conclusion) and essays (introduction, body paragraphs, conclusion) and of course students should be familiar with these basics. However, there is a danger to over-emphasizing standard, cut 'n' paste organizational structures. During a curriculum development workshop on writing, one teacher brought in stacks and stacks of graphic organizers, and regaled us as to how she drilled her students into perfect mastery of the "hamburger" approach to essay construction. But then she ended by complaining that, now that the students knew the "hamburger" cold, they refused to try any other structure, and their writing was deadly boring as a result.

ELL students are likely to hold tenaciously to something that they know works, suggesting that the cookie-cutter approach is only a good idea if you want cookie-cutter writing. If you want to encourage *writers*, tackle Organization as a trait inherently linked to the subject and intent of each individual task. If a student is providing directions, it makes sense to deliver the directions in the order that they should be completed. If the student is defending an argument, the relative strengths of each point she has to make will dictate the order in which they should be presented. In the storytelling exercises below, try modeling and encouraging students to tell the story in an unconventional way. Again, point up unique and successful organizational structures in the class reading assignments as well.

Model Lesson 4 – Introducing Organization

Content Objective: Students will be able to describe how the organization of a piece of writing is crucial to its effective communication.

Language Objective: Students will be able to define the trait of organization. Students will be able to identify how shifts in organization affect the quality of a written piece.

Building Background/Connecting With Prior Knowledge:
Hand students the two samples below and the rubrics for Ideas and Word Choice. Ask them to use the rubrics to evaluate and compare both pieces. This activity can work individually or in groups.

Sample 1
How to Turn on My Coffee Maker

You begin by placing coffee grounds in the top of the coffee maker and filling it up with water. Then you turn the knob to "brew" and… nothing happens. When the coffee maker clock moves to 8:31pm, the machine will turn on by itself, and finally you will have coffee. If it doesn't work, then you have to look at the time on the coffee maker's clock. For example, the clock might say "8:30pm." You now need to turn the knob to "program" and set the time for the coffee maker to automatically turn on to "8:31pm." Then you need to turn the knob to "automatic." My coffee maker is a little bit broken. It makes coffee, but it's difficult to get it to start. This is not the real time, but it is important that you remember whatever time the clock says. Well, sometimes it works and sometimes it doesn't.

Sample 2
How to Turn on My Coffee Maker

My coffee maker is a little bit broken. It makes coffee, but it's difficult to get it to start. You begin by placing coffee grounds in the top and filling it up with water. Then you turn the knob to "brew" and... nothing happens. Well, sometimes it works and sometimes it doesn't. If it doesn't work, then you have to look at the time on the coffee maker's clock. This is not the real time, but it is important that you remember whatever time the clock says. For example, the clock might say "8:30pm." You now need to turn the knob to "program" and set the time for the coffee maker to automatically turn on to "8:31pm." Then you need to turn the knob to "automatic." When the coffee maker clock moves to 8:31pm, the machine will turn on by itself, and finally you will have coffee.

Of course, what we're hoping for here is that the students quickly observe that the ideas and the word choice are exactly the same, but that Sample 2 is easier to understand than Sample 1. Now you need to discuss why. If students don't immediately identify that Sample 1 is told out of order, prompt them to tell you exactly how the two pieces are different, and lead them from there.

Teacher Input/Guided Practice:

Tell the students that the trait of Organization is all about the order in which things are written. Use the Coffee Maker samples to emphasize how Organization and Ideas are not the same thing: it is possible to have a perfectly good Idea, but convey it imperfectly because of poor Organization.

To further illustrate the notion of Organization, you will be dividing your students into three groups, then giving them sentence strips with sections of a sample of writing on them for the students to put in order. One group will work on a set of instructions, one group will work on a story, and one group will work on a brief problem-solution essay. If you'd like to differentiate a little bit, note that the instructions are probably the easiest task, while the problem-solution essay will be the most challenging.

Create sentence strips for each bullet:

Instructions
- How to Open a Locker
- First you look at your locker combinations. It should be three numbers.
- Start with the first number. Turn the lock dial to the right until the arrow points to the first number.
- Next, turn the lock dial to the left. Go past the second number one time, then stop on the second number the second time.
- Finally, turn the dial to right and stop on the third number. Your locker should open now.

Story

- Once upon a time there was a little girl carrying a basket of food to her grandmother, who lived in the woods. As the little girl walked through the woods, a wolf saw her.
- The wolf decided he wanted to steal the food. He ran ahead to the grandmother's house.
- The wolf ate the grandmother, put on her clothes, and got into her bed.
- The little girl came into her grandmother's house and went to the old lady's room. The little girl could see that it was a wolf pretending to be her grandmother.
- The wolf jumped out of the bed and tried to eat the little girl. A man was outside cutting trees. He ran in, chopped the wolf up with his axe, and let the grandmother out of the wolf's stomach.
- The grandmother and the little girl lived happily ever after.

Problem-Solution Essay

- Too many deer live in a neighborhood just outside the city.
- People in the neighborhood like the deer and put corn out in their yard for the deer to eat.
- The deer like the corn, and stay near the houses to get the free food.
- There is not enough room for all the deer. As a result, deer can't find enough food in the woods and are very small. Also, the deer often run into the roads and get hit by cars.
- The people in the neighborhood should stop feeding corn to the deer and let the deer move away from the houses. It would be safer for the deer in the long run.

Scramble up each group's sentence strips, then ask the groups to assemble them in order. If possible, have them tape the results up on a wall or on the board. Each group will also have to explain their reasons for their final decisions. If students get a piece out of order, ask the other groups to help move it, but expect them to explain why they are moving it.

When the students are done, provide your own commentary on the order. If they were able to post the sentence strips on the board, you can even write out labels to reinforce what you're saying. Note that the instructions follow the first-next-last order. The story follows a traditional plot arc: introduction/scene setting, rising action, conflict, climax/conflict resolution, denouement. Also note the presence of the traditional "once upon a time" and "happily ever after." Nothing wrong with signposts! For the problem-solution essay, note that the problem is laid out first, and that the biggest idea comes first, followed by details. Then the essay is ended with a statement of the solution.

Provide students with a copy of the student-friendly Organizational rubric. Ask them read the rubric and tell you what the rubric says they must have (answer: a beginning and an end, order) in order to do a good job with Organization.

Review for Mastery:

Remind students again that Ideas and Organization are separate traits. In fact, to prove it, the class will now write a story (or a set of instructions, whichever works for you) that uses the dumbest, dullest, lamest idea ever, but has a beginning and an end, and good order.

Work with the whole class to think of a terrible idea for the topic, then write out the piece on the board – prompting the students with "how should we start?" or "are you sure this is what happens next?" until the story is complete. Then ask students to rate the final piece using their new rubric.

Success Descriptors

Not Yet	Emerging	Effective	Strong
No organizational structure is present.	An organizational structure to the writing is starting to emerge with either a beginning, an end, or perhaps both present.	An obvious organizational structure is present; a beginning, middle, and an end are present and all connected with logical transitions.	A creative, strong flow to the writing results from an internal organization that draws the reader in and then moves him/her through the piece from beginning to end.

Trait: Conventions

The trait of Conventions refers to the demesne of the copy-editor: punctuation, spelling and syntax. As your students are still only fledgling English-users, perfectionism is not the goal at this point. Your focus should be on the students' execution of spelling, grammar and punctuation that has already been explicitly taught in your classroom. Any further consideration should only be related to how badly the mistakes obscure the meaning of the response.

Model Lesson 5 – Introducing the Trait of Conventions

Content Objective: Students will be able to apply what they are learning about English spelling, punctuation and grammar to their writing tasks. Students will be able to discuss how observing conventions improves the readability of their writing.

Language Objectives: Students will be able to define Conventions as a trait of good writing. Students will be able to explain how poor punctuation, capitalization and spelling hinder the effectiveness of writing. Students will be able to employ correct capitalization and punctuation, and to identify spelling mistakes and correct them with the help of a dictionary.

Connecting With the Objectives/Connecting With Prior Knowledge:
As a quiet warm-up, write the following questions on the board and have students write the answers on their own:
- Name the three traits of good writing we have studied so far: (Ideas, Word Choice, Organization)
- What do you think the name of the trait we're learning about today will be? (Conventions)
- What do you think "conventions" means?

Teacher Input:

Prepare index cards with responses provided below. On the back of each card, write the letter associated with the response nice and large. You will be handing out the cards to individual students and asking them to read what is on their card when you prompt them. The letter on the back of the card will help you keep track of who has which card.

This exercise is to illustrate the exact meaning of the word "convention" – a basic rule of interaction or performance that everyone is expected to follow so that everyone knows what's going on. The students with the cards will be saying certain conventional phrases that are part of everyday interaction, while you deliver inappropriate responses.

Student Card	**Your Response**
A. Hi, how are you?	A. Horrible.
B. Good morning!	B. No, I won't.
C. Thank you very much.	C. Never mind.
D. Hi, my name is _____.	D. Goodbye!
E. A-choo! (sneeze)	E. Don't sneeze!
F. Ring! Ring! (as a telephone)	F. Are you there?

Hopefully the students get the idea. Perhaps they may even laugh or try to correct you. Once you've been through all six cards, ask them what is wrong. They should tell you that your answers were all wrong. Point out that "Horrible" and "Don't sneeze!" are logical responses. Ask students to tell you the "right" responses:

Student Card	**Right Response**
A. Hi, how are you?	A. Fine! How are you?
B. Good morning!	B. Morning!
C. Thank you very much.	C. You're welcome.
D. Hi, my name is _____.	D. Nice to meet you, ___. My name is ___.
E. A-choo! (sneeze)	E. Bless you!
F. Ring! Ring! (as a telephone)	F. Hello?

While "bless you" makes, frankly, less sense than "don't sneeze," it is the rule, or convention, that we say "bless you" and life works much smoother if we just follow the rule. A New Zealander always answers the phone with "Are you there?" (something about a long, painful history of spotty phone service), but that response will totally throw an American caller.

Tell the students that simple things like these are Conventions: basic rules that help everyone understand what is going on. There are conventions for speaking, and there are conventions for writing. Now share this:

Jany. 6th   I was up last night at 12 to right the Boat   the banks were Caveing in, which made it necessary to fix the pries frequently, this morning early I fixed the pries, and large Pees of the bank sliped in, which obliged all hands to, go Down & make all secure   I ordered those men who had fought got Drunk & neglected Duty to go and build a hut for a Woman who promises to wash & Sow &c. I Spoke to the men on the Subject of my order, U L with quade. to day was is 1° 1' 1" ad +   a hog found in the Prairie by some men & they Skined   I send out Shields to enquire in the neighbourhood whoes hog it was & inform me. Thermometer at, 12 oClock 31 above 0 at 4 oCk at 30° above (0)_

(from the journals of Lewis and Clark, 1804)

The journals of Lewis and Clark are great fun because neither one of those venerable gentlemen could spell their way out of a wet paper bag. Note also the creative use of the comma in the sentence "…and large Pees of the bank sliped in, which obliged all hands to, go Down & make all secure."   And actually the period at the end there is mine, not Mr. Clark's. Fantastic stuff.

Highlight, for your students:
- caveing
- Pees
- sliped
- sow
- skined
- whoes

Tell students that, at this time, there really wasn't any such thing as a complete English dictionary, and that many educated writers spelled words however they thought best. The idea of having everyone spell all words the same way was just coming into fashion when the Lewis and Clark expedition set out. So why is spelling all words the same a good idea?

Note also the abbreviations Clark uses:
- Jany (for Jan., or January)
- &c (for etc., or etcetera)
- oCk (for o'clock)

Discuss how it is important that abbreviations be conventional as well, or nobody will understand what you're trying to say (as "U L with quade. to day was is 1° 1' 1" ad +" so aptly illustrates).

The purpose of writing is to clearly convey ideas, so if the two people sharing ideas don't follow the same rules, the conventions, the ideas can't come through clearly.

Guided Practice:

Have students read each section below, then circle what types of errors are found in each selection:

We slept in a large dormitory in white enameled iron bedsteads The girls against the east wall and the boys against the west After lights out Matron would sit in a chair by the door her knitting needles *click click clicking* away to make sure we didn't try to whisper or get up

spelling   punctuation   capitalization

Their was hardly any need. You lerned soon enuff not to get two close to anyone, bicaus chances are thay wood be gone within the week. I made the mistek of becoming fond of a boy named Andy, only to see him dragged away after forgeting to smile during dress rehersal.

spelling   punctuation   capitalization

besides, we were always exhausted by lights-out. we were awoken at 4:00, expected at morning chants by 4:15, then calisthenics, a breakfast of ovaltine and gruel at 5:30, dance and singing practice in the dojo until 11:00, a thirty minute break for lunch, generally some sort of stew, then rehearsal or filming for however long it took. none of the children recieved dinner until the mr. hopkins, the director was pleased with the performance or wrapped the take. one night i remember singing and dancing to "skip to my lou" for eleven hours straight and finally being allowed our bread-and-butter and fish sticks at nearly midnight.

spelling   punctuation   capitalization

Review for Mastery:

As a ticket out, either orally or written, students must give an example of a writing convention (spelling, punctuation, capitalization) and finish this sentence:

Being careful to have good Conventions in your writing is important because

_____.

Success Descriptors

Not Yet	Emerging	Effective	Strong
No evidence of correct conventions is present.	Some words are capitalized or punctuated correctly; most are not.	Capitalization & punctuation are mostly correct. Spelling is usually right. Grammar & usage are still very weak.	Capitalization, punctuation, spelling, and grammar usage are strong and usually correct. Little editing would be required to make this piece perfect.

Chapter 2 Activities

In this section, students will be asked to respond using five different formats. The formats are grouped together so that the students may become comfortable with each one through practice. You will need to model examples as you introduce each format.

The first format is to caption a picture. The students will be asked to write a sentence (they can write more if they get inspired!) in response to an existing photograph. To model a response, find a high-interest photograph that tells a story or could elicit an interesting description, show it to the students, then talk your way through creating a sentence about it. Identify objects and actions in the photograph, make notes about them on the board, then pull them together into a simple sentence.

If you feel it is necessary, you may want to discuss each picture orally with the class before they do their entries, and work with them to come up with words they might use to discuss each picture.

The second format will be the storyboard. Students are presented with three frames, blanks underneath the frames, and a topic about which to write. The students are to draw pictures in the frames that tell the story, then write a sentence below each frame that says what is going on in words. The prompts are a little vague, because the students need to use their heads and create their own story, then think about how they will break it down on the page. You will want to model this, perhaps more than once.

To model responding to storyboard prompts, draw the three frames and the blanks on your board (or on a poster board to be saved for future reference). Write your prompt on the board:

Have you ever lost something? Use the boxes to draw what happened when you lost something. Write what happens in each box in the lines below that box.

In the first box draw you looking frantic (for the stick-figure cadre, this would involve round eyes and sweat drops flying off the head) and a thought bubble featuring the object that has been lost. In the second box draw you looking in a likely spot. In the third box, draw you triumphantly (big smile, lines radiating from the head to denote a glow of joy) holding the lost object, standing next to the place where it was found.

Your sentences—which you will talk through generating, pointing out "I," the object of concern, and what you are doing – should read along the lines of: "I can't find _____." "I look for _____." "I find _____."

Dialogues are the third format of prompt response. The students will be presented with a conversation they might have and dialogue balloons in which to write what is said in the conversation. You will want to have taught questions at this point, as all of the responses will require the students to write a question or two. A great reference for this would be dialogues presented in your ESL newcomers' textbook.

To model responding to a dialogue prompt, reproduce the dialogue bubbles as they appear on the entry page on your board or poster-board. Write the following prompt: *You see that your friend is eating chocolate candies. You love chocolate candies and want to eat a piece. Write what you and your friend say when you talk about the candy.* Label the three balloons pointing to the left "FRIEND" and label the two balloons pointing to the right "YOU." Talk through and transcribe a conversation similar to:

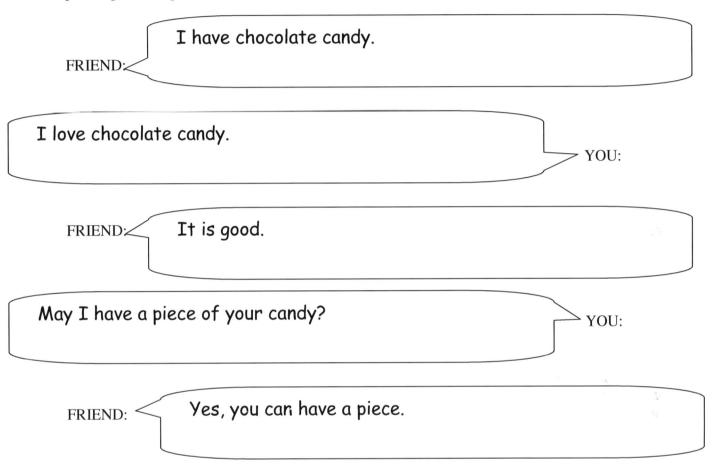

FRIEND: I have chocolate candy.

I love chocolate candy. YOU:

FRIEND: It is good.

May I have a piece of your candy? YOU:

FRIEND: Yes, you can have a piece.

Emphasize that you are filling the dialogue bubbles with what each person SAYS, not with what they do or think.

The fourth response format is the Instructional Diagram. The process is slightly different for this section: students will be given a list of eight topics from which they may choose any four to complete their entries. The expectation is that the student will use pictures and words to describe a "how-to" process. Complete sentences are not the focus for these entries, but rather the sequencing of ideas and how they lay it all out on paper.

Consider the following as a model:

How do you microwave a frozen pizza?

Your diagram could include the following pictures: pulling pizza out of the freezer, taking pizza out of the packaging, placing pizza in the microwave, pressing buttons on the microwave, waiting, and pulling out the sizzling pizza.

Next to the pictures you could write the directions: *Take the pizza out of the freezer. Open the box. Put the pizza in the microwave. Enter the time on the microwave. Take out your cooked pizza and enjoy!*

The final format for Section Two is the Note format. Think of these responses as both proto-letters and proto-paragraphs. All you will really need to model, as such, is the "Dear...." and the "Sincerely...." parts. It will be more important to discuss vocabulary and build a little background about each situation before letting the students tackle each entry. With this format, Conventions and Organization are the sole focus for evaluation, and you will want to review vocabulary, grammar and punctuation learned to date, and explore basic organizational concepts such as beginning with your Big Point, then filling in details, and ending with a conclusive statement.

On the following page is a student friendly presentation of the Traits evaluation in Section Two and their descriptors. Please review this with your students and remind them to refer to it as they work.

Student-Friendly Rubric: Section Two

TRAIT	Not Yet	Emerging	Effective	Strong
Ideas	You didn't answer the question. Your answer was not about the question.	You tried to answer the question, but you could have said more.	Answer the question – write about what you were told to write about. Write as many things as you can.	Answer the question with new, interesting ideas that no one else thought of. Tell more than the prompt asks you to tell.
Organization	What you said had no order to it.	Your answer had a beginning and an end, but you didn't put everything in the best order.	Your answer has a beginning and an end. You say things in the order that they happen.	The order that you choose to write things is the best and most interesting way to give your answer.
Word Choice	You did not use English words. The English words you did use were not the right words and did not say what you wanted to say.	Some of the words you used were not the best English words to say what you wanted to say.	Use English words that you have learned. Check your dictionary for words you don't know. Use words you know correctly.	Use new words that you haven't studied yet and use them correctly – try your dictionary! See what works!
Conventions	You did not write complete sentences with a subject and a verb. You did not capitalize the first letters of your sentences. You did not put a punctuation mark at the end of your sentences. You made spelling mistakes that made it very hard to read your words.	You remembered to capitalize and punctuate, but you made some mistakes. You did not match your verbs to your subjects. Some of your sentences were not complete. Some of your words were spelled wrong.	You write complete sentences with a subject and a verb. You begin your sentences with capital letters. You end your sentences with a period (.), question mark (?) or exclamation point (!). You make your verbs agree with your subject. You spell the words you know correctly.	You did not make any mistakes.

Entry 1
Write a sentence about what you see in this picture.

_____

_____

Trait Assessment
Trait: Ideas
Success Descriptors (Circle one and add your own comments)

Not Yet	Emerging	Effective	Strong
Does not answer prompt or it is not possible to understand how response relates to prompt.	Single words or phrases reflect an attempt to answer prompt. Sentences are attempted, but one has to work to understand their relation to the prompt.	Simple sentences use subject and action to relay response to prompt.	Sentences clearly relay response to prompt, and student presents ideas that develop further on the scope of the prompt.
Comments: _____ _____ _____	Comments: _____ _____ _____	Comments: _____ _____ _____	Comments: _____ _____ _____

Entry 2
Write a sentence about what you see in this picture.

_____

_____

Trait Assessment
Trait: Word Choice
Success Descriptors (Circle one and add your own comments)

Not Yet	Emerging	Effective	Strong
Does not respond to prompt. Does not respond in English. It is not possible to understand how response relates to prompt.	Responds to prompt, but some words may not be in English or may not be accurate choices.	Responds to prompt, uses all English, words are accurate in meaning.	Responds to prompt, words are all appropriate choices in terms of meaning. Student attempts to use sophisticated vocabulary and attempts are comprehensible.
Comments: _____ _____ _____	Comments: _____ _____ _____	Comments: _____ _____ _____	Comments: _____ _____ _____

Entry 3
Write a sentence about what you see in this picture.

_____

_____

Trait Assessment
Trait: Word Choice
Success Descriptors (Circle one and add your own comments)

Not Yet	Emerging	Effective	Strong
Does not respond to prompt. Does not respond in English. It is not possible to understand how response relates to prompt.	Responds to prompt, but some words may not be in English or may not be accurate choices.	Responds to prompt, uses all English, words are accurate in meaning.	Responds to prompt, words are all appropriate choices in terms of meaning. Student attempts to use sophisticated vocabulary and attempts are comprehensible.
Comments: _____ _____ _____	Comments: _____ _____ _____	Comments: _____ _____ _____	Comments: _____ _____ _____

Entry 4

Write a sentence about what you see in this picture.

Trait Assessment
Trait: Conventions
Success Descriptors (Circle one and add your own comments)

Not Yet	Emerging	Effective	Strong
Does not answer prompt. No capitalization or punctuation is in evidence.	Initial words are capitalized, sentences end with ending punctuation, although a few mistakes in punctuation, spelling and conjugation may have occurred.	All initial words are capitalized, all sentences end with ending punctuation. Only one or two mistakes in spelling may occur. Conjugation is attempted with understanding of the form, but minor mistakes may occur.	No mistakes in capitalization, punctuation, spelling or conjugation.
Comments: _____ _____ _____	Comments: _____ _____ _____	Comments: _____ _____ _____	Comments: _____ _____ _____

Entry 5

What would you do on a perfect vacation? Use the three boxes below to show where you would go and the different things you would do. Write a sentence about what is happening in each box on the lines below the box.

Trait Assessment
Trait: Ideas
Success Descriptors (Circle one and add your own comments)

Not Yet	Emerging	Effective	Strong
Does not answer prompt or it is not possible to understand how response relates to prompt.	Single words or phrases reflect an attempt to answer prompt. Sentences are attempted, but one has to work to understand their relation to the prompt.	Simple sentences use subject and action to relay response to prompt.	Sentences clearly relay response to prompt, and student presents ideas that develop further on the scope of the prompt.
Comments: _____ _____ _____	Comments: _____ _____ _____	Comments: _____ _____ _____	Comments: _____ _____ _____

Entry 6

Re-tell a children's story or joke that you love. Use the three boxes below to draw what happens. Write a sentence about what happens in each box on the lines below that box.

_____   _____   _____

_____   _____   _____

_____   _____   _____

Trait Assessment
Trait: Organization
Success Descriptors (Circle one and add your own comments)

Not Yet	Emerging	Effective	Strong
Does not respond to prompt.	A beginning and end is clear, however, there is no further attempt at relating a structure to the ideas presented.	The ideas are presented in an order that makes sense to the answering of the prompt.	The order of presentation chosen for the ideas is ideal for clear expression of those ideas.
Comments: _____ _____ _____	Comments: _____ _____ _____	Comments: _____ _____ _____	Comments: _____ _____ _____

Entry 7
Tell a story about a fight. Use the three boxes below to draw what happens. Write a sentence about what happens in each box on the lines below that box.

_____   _____   _____

_____   _____   _____

_____   _____   _____

Trait Assessment
Trait: Conventions
Success Descriptors (Circle one and add your own comments)

Not Yet	Emerging	Effective	Strong
Does not answer prompt. No capitalization or punctuation is in evidence.	Initial words are capitalized, sentences end with ending punctuation, although a few mistakes in punctuation, spelling and conjugation may have occurred.	All initial words are capitalized, all sentences end with ending punctuation. Only one or two mistakes in spelling may occur. Conjugation is attempted with understanding of the form, but minor mistakes may occur.	No mistakes in capitalization, punctuation, spelling or conjugation.
Comments: _____ _____ _____	Comments: _____ _____ _____	Comments: _____ _____ _____	Comments: _____ _____ _____

Entry 8

Tell a story about how you helped somebody. . Use the three boxes below to draw what happens. Write a sentence about what happens in each box on the lines below that box.

Trait Assessment
Trait: Word Choice
Success Descriptors (Circle one and add your own comments)

Not Yet	Emerging	Effective	Strong
Does not respond to prompt. Does not respond in English. It is not possible to understand how response relates to prompt.	Responds to prompt, but some words may not be in English or may not be accurate choices.	Responds to prompt, uses all English, words are accurate in meaning.	Responds to prompt, words are all appropriate choices in terms of meaning. Student attempts to use sophisticated vocabulary and attempts are comprehensible.
Comments: _____ _____ _____	Comments: _____ _____ _____	Comments: _____ _____ _____	Comments: _____ _____ _____

Entry 9

You meet a new student. His name is Hector and he is from El Salvador. In the dialogue balloons, write what you and Hector say to each other when you meet.

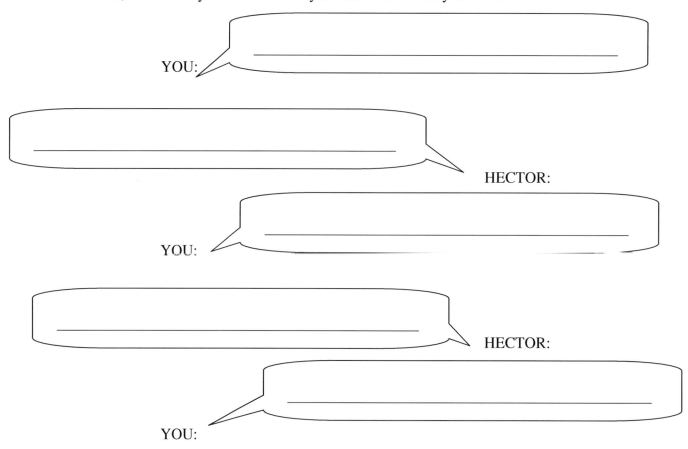

YOU:

HECTOR:

YOU:

HECTOR:

YOU:

Trait Assessment
Trait: Organization
Success Descriptors (Circle one and add your own comments)

Not Yet	Emerging	Effective	Strong
Does not respond to prompt.	A beginning and end is clear, however, there is no further attempt at relating a structure to the ideas presented.	The ideas are presented in an order that makes sense to the answering of the prompt.	The order of presentation chosen for the ideas is ideal for clear expression of those ideas.
Comments: _____ _____ _____	Comments: _____ _____ _____	Comments: _____ _____ _____	Comments: _____ _____ _____

Entry 10

You want to ask a friend to do something fun with you. Tell your friend what you want to do. Have your friend ask a question about what you will do, then write your answer. Then write what your friend says – does your friend want to go?

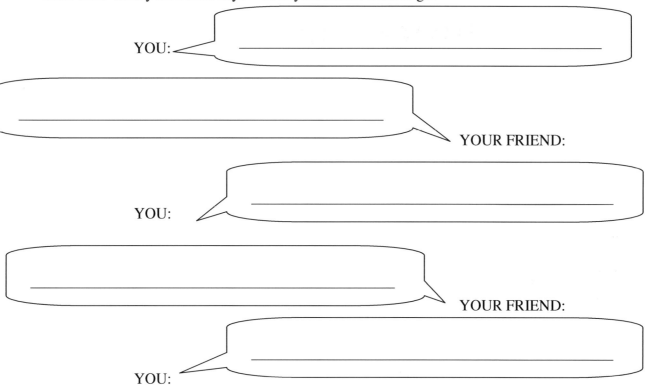

\Trait Assessment
Trait: Word Choice
Success Descriptors (Circle one and add your own comments)

Not Yet	Emerging	Effective	Strong
Does not respond to prompt. Does not respond in English. It is not possible to understand how response relates to prompt.	Responds to prompt, but some words may not be in English or may not be accurate choices.	Responds to prompt, uses all English, words are accurate in meaning.	Responds to prompt, words are all appropriate choices in terms of meaning. Student attempts to use sophisticated vocabulary and attempts are comprehensible.
Comments: _____ _____ _____	Comments: _____ _____ _____	Comments: _____ _____ _____	Comments: _____ _____ _____

Entry 11

You did not finish your homework last night, and you need to talk to your teacher about this. Tell your teacher that you did not finish. Have your teacher ask why. Explain to your teacher. Write what your teacher says – are you in trouble? Will you be able to turn in your homework late?

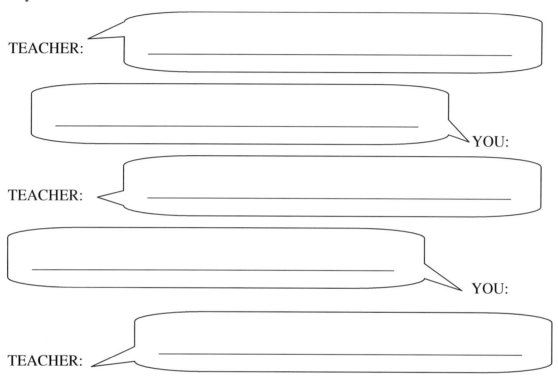

TEACHER: _____

YOU: _____

TEACHER: _____

YOU: _____

TEACHER: _____

Trait Assessment
Trait: Ideas
Success Descriptors (Circle one and add your own comments)

Not Yet	Emerging	Effective	Strong
Does not answer prompt or it is not possible to understand how response relates to prompt.	Single words or phrases reflect an attempt to answer prompt. Sentences are attempted, but one has to work to understand their relation to the prompt.	Simple sentences use subject and action to relay response to prompt.	Sentences clearly relay response to prompt, and student presents ideas that develop further on the scope of the prompt.
Comments: _____ _____	Comments: _____ _____	Comments: _____ _____	Comments: _____ _____

Entry 12

Something important has happened in the news. Tell a friend about it. Have your friend ask questions about it, and then tell them more.

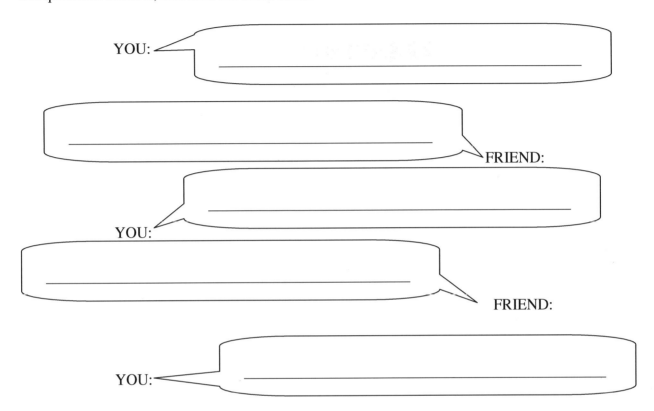

Trait Assessment
Trait: Conventions
Success Descriptors (Circle one and add your own comments)

Not Yet	Emerging	Effective	Strong
Does not answer prompt. No capitalization or punctuation is in evidence.

Comments:
_____
_____ | Initial words are capitalized, sentences end with ending punctuation, although a few mistakes in punctuation, spelling and conjugation may have occurred.

Comments: _____
_____ | All initial words are capitalized, all sentences end with ending punctuation. Only one or two mistakes in spelling may occur. Conjugation is attempted with understanding of the form, but minor mistakes may occur.

Comments: _____
_____ | No mistakes in capitalization, punctuation, spelling or conjugation.

Comments:
_____
_____ |

Entries 13-16

You will explain how to do something. In the box provided on the next few pages, draw pictures that show how to do something, and write sentences with the pictures that explain.

These are the topics you may choose from. Choose one different topic for each entry. Write the topic in the blank at the top of the entry.

- How do you make a sandwich?

- How do you address an envelope?

- How do you open a locker?

- How do you tie a shoe?

- How do you draw your favorite cartoon character?

- How do you turn on a computer and get on the Internet?

- How do you order a burger at a fast-food restaurant drive-through window?

- How do you wash dishes?

Entry 13

How do _____?

Trait Assessment
Trait: Ideas
Success Descriptors (Circle one and add your own comments)

Not Yet	Emerging	Effective	Strong
Does not answer prompt or it is not possible to understand how response relates to prompt.	Single words or phrases reflect an attempt to answer prompt. Sentences are attempted, but one has to work to understand their relation to the prompt.	Simple sentences use subject and action to relay response to prompt.	Sentences clearly relay response to prompt, and student presents ideas that develop further on the scope of the prompt.
Comments: _____ _____ _____	Comments: _____ _____ _____	Comments: _____ _____ _____	Comments: _____ _____ _____

Entry 14

How do _____ ?

Trait Assessment
Trait: Word Choice
Success Descriptors (Circle one and add your own comments)

Not Yet	Emerging	Effective	Strong
Does not respond to prompt. Does not respond in English. It is not possible to understand how response relates to prompt.	Responds to prompt, but some words may not be in English or may not be accurate choices.	Responds to prompt, uses all English, words are accurate in meaning.	Responds to prompt, words are all appropriate choices in terms of meaning. Student attempts to use sophisticated vocabulary and attempts are comprehensible.
Comments: _____ _____ _____	Comments: _____ _____ _____	Comments: _____ _____ _____	Comments: _____ _____ _____

Entry 15

How do _____?

Trait Assessment
Trait: Organization
Success Descriptors (Circle one and add your own comments)

Not Yet	Emerging	Effective	Strong
Does not respond to prompt.	A beginning and end is clear, however, there is no further attempt at relating a structure to the ideas presented.	The ideas are presented in an order that makes sense to the answering of the prompt.	The order of presentation chosen for the ideas is ideal for clear expression of those ideas.
Comments: _____ _____	Comments: _____ _____	Comments: _____ _____	Comments: _____ _____

Entry 16

How do _____ ?

Trait Assessment
Trait: Ideas
Success Descriptors (Circle one and add your own comments)

Not Yet	Emerging	Effective	Strong
Does not answer prompt or it is not possible to understand how response relates to prompt.	Single words or phrases reflect an attempt to answer prompt. Sentences are attempted, but one has to work to understand their relation to the prompt.	Simple sentences use subject and action to relay response to prompt.	Sentences clearly relay response to prompt, and student presents ideas that develop further on the scope of the prompt.
Comments: _____ _____ _____	Comments: _____ _____ _____	Comments: _____ _____ _____	Comments: _____ _____ _____

Entry 17

You are going out with a friend to have some fun. Write a note to your family to explain where you are going, who you are with, what you are doing, and when you will be back.

_____

_____

_____

_____

_____

_____

_____

_____

_____

_____

_____

_____

Trait: Conventions
Success Descriptors (Circle one and add your own comments)

Not Yet	Emerging	Effective	Strong
Does not answer prompt. No capitalization or punctuation is in evidence. Comments: _____ _____ _____	Initial words are capitalized, sentences end with ending punctuation, although a few mistakes in punctuation, spelling and conjugation may have occurred. Comments: _____ _____ _____	All initial words are capitalized, all sentences end with ending punctuation. Only one or two mistakes in spelling may occur. Conjugation is attempted with understanding of the form, but minor mistakes may occur. Comments: _____ _____ _____	No mistakes in capitalization, punctuation, spelling or conjugation. Comments: _____ _____ _____

Entry 18

You did not come to school yesterday because you were sick. Write a note to your teacher to explain why you did not come to school. Also tell your teacher what you will do to finish any work that you missed.

_____

_____

_____

_____

_____

_____

_____

_____

_____

_____

_____

Trait Assessment
Trait: Organization
Success Descriptors (Circle one and add your own comments)

Not Yet	Emerging	Effective	Strong
Does not respond to prompt.	A beginning and end is clear, however, there is no further attempt at relating a structure to the ideas presented.	The ideas are presented in an order that makes sense to the answering of the prompt.	The order of presentation chosen for the ideas is ideal for clear expression of those ideas.
Comments: _____ _____ _____	Comments: _____ _____ _____	Comments: _____ _____ _____	Comments: _____ _____ _____

Entry 19

You know all about something important that happened at your school. Write a note to the editor* of your school newspaper and tell her that you want to write a story for the newspaper about the important thing that happened.

_____

_____

_____

_____

_____

_____

_____

_____

_____

_____

_____

_____

Trait: Conventions

Success Descriptors (Circle one and add your own comments)

Not Yet	Emerging	Effective	Strong
Does not answer prompt. No capitalization or punctuation is in evidence.

Comments:
_____
_____
_____ | Initial words are capitalized, sentences end with ending punctuation, although a few mistakes in punctuation, spelling and conjugation may have occurred.

Comments: _____
_____
_____ | All initial words are capitalized, all sentences end with ending punctuation. Only one or two mistakes in spelling may occur. Conjugation is attempted with understanding of the form, but minor mistakes may occur.

Comments: _____
_____
_____ | No mistakes in capitalization, punctuation, spelling or conjugation.

Comments:
_____
_____
_____ |

*editor: *the person who is in charge of a newspaper. Editors decide which stories will be used and can change, or* edit *the articles that the writers turn in.*

Entry 20

You want to get a job at a clothes store. Write a note to the manager of the clothes store. Tell him you want to do the job. Tell him why you would do a good job.

_____

_____

_____

_____

_____

_____

_____

_____

_____

_____

_____

_____

Trait Assessment

Trait: Organization

Success Descriptors (Circle one and add your own comments)

Not Yet	Emerging	Effective	Strong
Does not respond to prompt.	A beginning and end is clear, however, there is no further attempt at relating a structure to the ideas presented.	The ideas are presented in an order that makes sense to the answering of the prompt.	The order of presentation chosen for the ideas is ideal for clear expression of those ideas.
Comments: _____ _____ _____	Comments: _____ _____ _____	Comments: _____ _____ _____	Comments: _____ _____ _____

Section Three:
Complex Sentences

To the teacher:

Before tackling Section Three, students should be confident in writing basic sentences, and should have learned about the grammar rules that enable one to write more complex sentences: conjunctions, prepositions and modifiers. In this section, students will be challenged to express complete ideas and more complex concepts, and to explore new frontiers in the use of English.

Trait: Sentence Fluency

The new Trait evaluated in this section is Sentence Fluency. It's no accident that there are two words in this trait name, because both have equal – yet independent – importance. High-quality evocations of this trait should include *sentences* that are varied, grammatically correct, and appropriate to the mode of expression. Beyond that, the work should have *fluency*: the flow and rhythm of the sentence construction should be enjoyable and should add to the expression of the piece.

The nice thing about Sentence Fluency is that I can tell you quite succinctly how to look for it: if a piece sounds good when read aloud, it has good Sentence Fluency. Simple as that.

However, the instruction of this trait is a little more involved. Add in the struggles of the English learner merely to get the verbs conjugated and the adjectives in the right place, and you have a real bugbear on your hands. There are several things you should keep in mind to help focus your approach:

- Before beginning work on this, give the students a good pile of tools for their sentence-construction toolbox: work with them on ways to extend and rearrange sentences and build their confidence there first.
- Remind students of the tools in their toolboxes when embarking on an assignment, but do not over-emphasize – for example, don't insist that they use compound sentences because you just studied compound sentences. Using a sentence structure for the sake of using it will assuredly kill the Fluency element.
- Consign syntax and grammar mistakes to the realm of Conventions. For an ELL student, the sentence, "In the room pink the princess brush his hair." has problems with Conventions, not necessarily with Sentence Fluency. Remember that an advantage of the Traits process is that, by keeping to one trait lane at a time, you can avoid overwhelming students with the mistakes that are naturally going to come with language acquisition.

Reading well and revising wisely will help as much with this trait as any other, which is nifty, because reading well and revising wisely (and often) is how the pros do it. When you read aloud a particularly mellifluous passage, pick it apart with your students to help them see how the author's choice of sentence structure and rhythm affects the flow of the reading.

Model Lesson 5 – Introducing Sentence Fluency

Content Objectives: Students will be able to describe some attributes of good sentence fluency and to understand how applying those attributes to their own writing will help to improve it.

Language Objectives: Students will be able to define Fluency as it applies to this trait. Students will be able to recognize various sentence structures.

Building Background/Connecting with Prior Knowledge:

Much of the main activity in this lesson is based on identifying subjects and verbs (as predicates). Most ESL instructional programs and mainstream secondary English language arts programs address this skill fairly early on. Ensure that your students have mastered subjects and verbs, and use a few minutes at the beginning of class here to review in a manner that recalls previous instruction.

Teacher Input/Guided Practice:

If possible, have students listen to a professional reading of the Gettysburg Address. Mpegs of readings by Jeff Daniels, Sam Waterston, and Johnny Cash are available at http://www.fifttesweb.com/usa/gettysburg-address.htm. I personally am partial to the Johnny Cash version. If playing a recorded version is not possible, read the address aloud to your students.

The Gettysburg Address is seminal in its brevity: it was an afterthought tacked on at the end of a two-hour-long speech by Judge Edward Everett and barely even noted at the time it was delivered. However, it is now hailed as one of the greatest American speeches of all time – not only for its sentiment, but for its unforgettable, elegant cadence. Students are asked to memorize this and deliver it aloud, not simply to read it for the meaning, and there is a reason for that.

After listening to the reading, ask students for their reflections, if any. Explain to them that part of the speech's enduring fame stems from how it sounds. Now the students will analyze why it sounds so good.

Provide students with the text of the Gettysburg Address:

Four score and seven years ago our fathers brought forth on this continent, a new nation, conceived in Liberty, and dedicated to the proposition that all men are created equal.

Now we are engaged in a great civil war, testing whether that nation, or any nation so conceived and so dedicated, can long endure. We are met on a great battlefield of that war. We have come to dedicate a portion of that field, as a final resting place for those who here gave their lives that that nation might live. It is altogether fitting and proper that we should do this.

But, in a larger sense, we cannot dedicate—we cannot consecrate—we cannot hallow—this ground. The brave men, living and dead, who struggled here, have consecrated it, far above our poor power to add or detract. The world will little note, nor long remember what we say here, but it can never forget what they did here. It is for us the living, rather, to be dedicated here to the unfinished work which they who fought here have thus far so nobly advanced. It is rather for us to be here dedicated to the great task remaining before us—that from these honored dead we take increased devotion to that cause for which they gave the last full measure of devotion—that we here highly resolve that these dead shall not have died in vain—that this nation, under God, shall have a new birth of freedom— and that government of the people, by the people, for the people, shall not perish from the earth.

Students will each need two different colored highlighters (or light-colored markers, map pencils) and a pen or pencil. Ask them to:

- Highlight each sentence in the speech in alternating colors.
- Circle all subject nouns or pronouns.
- Underline all predicate verbs.

The result should look like this:

Four score and seven years ago our fathers brought forth on this continent, a new nation, conceived in Liberty, and dedicated to the proposition that all men are created equal.

Now we are engaged in a great civil war, testing whether that nation, or any nation so conceived and so dedicated, can long endure. We are met on a great battlefield of that war. We have come to dedicate a portion of that field, as a final resting place for those who here gave their lives that that nation might live. It is altogether fitting and proper that we should do this.

But, in a larger sense, we cannot dedicate—we cannot consecrate—we cannot hallow—this ground. The brave men, living and dead, who struggled here, have consecrated it, far above our poor power to add or detract. The world will little note, nor long remember what we say here, but it can never forget what they did here. It is for us the living, rather, to be dedicated here to the unfinished work which they who fought here have thus far so nobly advanced. It is rather for us to be here dedicated to the great task remaining before us—that from these honored dead we take increased devotion to that cause for which they gave the last full measure of devotion—that we here highly resolve that these dead shall not have died in vain—that this nation, under God, shall have a new birth of freedom— and that government of the people, by the people, for the people, shall not perish from the earth.

Probably they won't have gotten this done perfectly, so go over the correct answers with the students before moving on to the analysis. Ask students to look at the list of statements below and mark which ones are true and which ones are false in regards to the Gettysburg Address.

- All of the sentences are long.
- There are long and short sentences.
- All of the sentences are short.

- All of the verbs are one word.
- All of the verbs are more than one word.
- Some verbs are one word and some verbs are more than one word.
- The subject is sometimes not the most important word in the sentence.
- The most important word in the sentence is always the subject.
- Not every sentence begins with the subject.
- Every sentence begins with the subject.

Now read out loud the following:

Our fathers created on this continent a new nation eighty-seven years ago. This nation was conceived in liberty. This nation was dedicated to the proposition that all men are created equal.

We are fighting a great civil war. We are testing whether our nation, or any nation like ours, can endure for long. We are met on a great battlefield of that war. We will dedicate a portion of that field as a final resting place for those who gave their lives here so that our nation could live. We should do this because it is altogether fitting and proper.

Point out that this version has sentences of a more uniform length, that all sentences begin with the subject, and that the verb lengths are kept under control. If it fits student ability and the time-frame, ask students to break down this version with highlighters, circles and lines as well to see the difference. Ask students to listen to the two different versions and offer opinions on which sounds better.

Tell the students that the difference they should be hearing lies in the trait of Sentence Fluency. Little of the vocabulary and none of the ideas or organization has been changed between the two versions, but the sentence structures have. The most obvious thing students should recognize is that having a variety of sentences is an important part of good Sentence Fluency.

The other part, the "Fluency" is more subjective. Point students to the sentence "But, in a larger sense, we cannot dedicate—we cannot consecrate—we cannot hallow—this ground." Why are there three whole verbs here? Why is the "we cannot" repeated? Does anyone notice the rhyme? Why did President Lincoln choose to phrase the sentence this way? Because it sounds *awesome*.

"It sounds awesome" is a bit subjective, but let's work with it. Write the following sentences on the board:

- I think trees look good.
- His car is fast and it looks cool.
- Pizza is yummy.
- Soccer is fun.
- When my girlfriend/boyfriend smiles it makes me happy.

Each student is to pick one sentence, and rewrite it so that it sounds awesome (or, at least, better than it does). If you would like to model, give them this:
- I think trees look good.

- I think that I shall never see/ a poem lovely as a tree. (Joyce Kilmer, "Trees")
- The tree is an angel that god sent down to watch over the earth. (Su Jung, *I am a Pencil*, p. 11)

Have students share out examples that they think worked out well.

Review for Mastery:

Remind students that for each trait that has been studied so far, a rubric for evaluating the trait on writing assignments has also been presented. Ask the students to work in small groups to write a rubric for Sentence Fluency. Give them this structure to fill in:

Not Yet	Emerging	Effective	Strong

Go over the student-friendly Sentence Fluency rubric and see how they did.

Success Descriptors

Not Yet	Emerging	Effective	Strong
Does not write in English. Does not write complete sentences. Does not write more than one sentence.	Two or more complete sentences are present, but there are problems with grammar or a repetitive sentence pattern.	Two or more complete sentences are present and are grammatically correct. There is variation in the sentence structures.	Two or more complete and correct sentences are present, there is variation in structure and that variation enhances the flow and readability of the piece.

At this point, what you are looking for are competent sentences and any variety at all. Keep in mind what types of sentences you have presented through direct instruction. As students have developed more skills in all areas at this point, the standards have been raised for several Traits:

Trait: Word Choice

Success Descriptors

Not Yet	Emerging	Effective	Strong
Does not write in English. Words are too inaccurate or badly spelled to determine meaning.	Words are simple and/or not the most accurate choice. Some inaccurate word choices are made.	Student uses familiar vocabulary to accurately convey his or her meaning.	Student attempts, with some success, to use new and sophisticated vocabulary to convey meaning

Students should be using taught vocabulary with confidence at this point, and should be familiar enough with their dictionaries to risk trying new words.

Trait: Ideas

Success Descriptors

Not Yet	Emerging	Effective	Strong
Does not answer prompt.	Most ideas address the prompt, but some are off-topic.	Ideas address the prompt to the degree requested.	Ideas address the prompt and extend beyond the degree requested. Student approaches the topic from a unique point of view.

There is a clear expectation that the student understands and answers the prompt. As the student's ability to express him- or herself has developed, the standards for the complexity and thoroughness of the response should be expanded.

Trait: Organization

Success Descriptors

Not Yet	Emerging	Effective	Strong
Student does not respond to prompt, does not include elements required by prompt, and/or no thought-out order is apparent in the response.	Sentences follow a logical order, but it is a simple order that does not reflect understanding of the need for organization specific to the prompt.	Sentences follow an order that is logical in responding to the prompt.	Organization is unique, creative, and enhances the meaning of the student's response.

This is the second section requiring multiple-sentence responses. Not only should a student now be able to arrange his or her thoughts in sequential order, but should also begin to understand that there are other organization patterns that are required for different writing assignments.

Trait: Conventions

Success Descriptors

Not Yet	Emerging	Effective	Strong
Not answered in English. Incomplete sentences. Failure to produce capitalization, ending punctuation. Spelling that renders the work incomprehensible.	Complete sentences. Capitalization and ending punctuation. Spelling, grammar, and interior punctuation errors occur but do not obscure the meaning of the response.	Complete sentences, capitalization, ending punctuation all present. No grammar mistakes in terms of conjugation, plurals, or articles. Grammar mistakes beyond direct-instruction do not obscure meaning. Minimal spelling errors.	Complete and complex sentences with no errors at all.

Notice that the Conventions bar has been raised as well. Basics such as capitalization and ending punctuation should be second nature by now. As you have introduced more complex grammar rules in your instruction, you should be expecting students to employ those rules correctly in production.

The first two prompts you will see in this section will be challenging students to explore English vocabulary and attempt to use more sophisticated words. The next two prompts are an "introduction" to Sentence Fluency, asking students to re-write paragraphs that originally consist of repetitive sentences. To model these first four prompts, do the first item in the prompt with the whole class.

The next six prompts (5-10) center on simple poetry. There are complete explanations of the poetry pattern and the required response in each prompt, but you will want to discuss these explanations with your students. It will be especially important to teach about rhymes and rhythm, and to explain to your students what the word "line" means in reference to a poem.

The following six prompts (11-16) are basic outlines that could later become short essays. To help students master the concepts of main ideas and supporting details, you will want to model your own responses to some of the prompts. What students should grasp here is that they begin with a sentence that lays out the Big Idea, then follow with details that relate to the Big Idea and expand on it.

The last four prompts (17-20) are "free writing." It's time to toss your kids out of the nest and make them compose complete responses on their own. When evaluating the responses to these prompts, focus on how well and completely the student answers the question. If organization is disingenuous, point the student to the outlines that the completed for Entries 11-16 and remind them about Big Ideas and supporting details. You very well may get a whole lotta rough and not too much in the way of diamonds, here, but look for those diamonds and encourage students to build on their existing success. We'll get more nit-picky about full paragraph responses in Section Four. Please refer your students to the Student-Friendly Rubric on the following page, to help them understand how to polish each Trait in this section.

Student-Friendly Rubric: Section Three

TRAITS	Not Yet	Emerging	Effective	Strong
Ideas	You didn't answer the question. Your answer was not about the question.	You tried to answer the question, but you could have said more.	Answer the question – write about what you were told to write about. Write as many things as you can.	Answer the question with new, interesting ideas that no one else thought of. Tell more than the prompt asks you to tell. You think of a new way to talk about the topic.
Organization	What you said had no order to it.	Your answer had a beginning and an end, but you didn't put everything in the best order.	Your answer has a beginning and an end. You say things in the order that they happen, or in an order that makes sense.	The order that you choose to write things is the best and most interesting way to give your answer.
Word Choice	You did not use English words. The English words you did use were not the right words and did not say what you wanted to say.	Some of the words you used were not the best English words to say what you wanted to say.	Use English words that you have learned. Check your dictionary for words you don't know. Use word you know correctly.	Use new words that you haven't studied yet and use them correctly – try your dictionary! See what works!
Sentence Fluency	You did not write complete sentences. You did not write more than one sentence. All of your sentences are simple and sound the same.	Some of your sentences were simple and many sentences followed the same pattern, sounded the same.	You try more complex sentences, you mix up long sentences and short sentences.	You choose the right style of sentence for what your are trying to say, you have different types of sentences. When you read your work out loud, it sounds good.
Conventions	You did not write complete sentences. You did not capitalize the first letters of your sentences. You did not put a punctuation mark at the end of your sentences. You made spelling mistakes that made it very hard to read your words.	You remembered to capitalize and punctuate, but you made some mistakes. You did not match your verbs to your subjects. Some of your words were spelled wrong.	You write complete sentences. You begin your sentences with capital letters. You end your sentences with the right punctuation mark. You make your verbs agree with your subject. You spell the words you know correctly.	You did not make any mistakes.

Entry 1

Read the following paragraph. The underlined words are very simple, and are not very interesting. Re-write the paragraph, and change as many of the underlined words as you can – use more interesting words that say more.

I like trees. Trees start as <u>little</u> seeds, then they <u>get big</u>. Trees have leaves that can be <u>many colors</u>. The leaves have <u>different shapes</u>. A <u>good</u> tree is a <u>big tree</u>.

_____

_____

_____

_____

_____

_____

_____

_____

_____

_____

Trait Assessment
Trait: Word Choice
Success Descriptors (Circle one and add your own comments)

Not Yet	Emerging	Effective	Strong
Does not write in English. Words are too inaccurate or badly spelled to determine meaning. Comments: _____ _____ _____	Words are simple and/or not the most accurate choice. Some inaccurate word choices are made. Comments: _____ _____ _____	Student uses familiar vocabulary to accurately convey his or her meaning. Comments: _____ _____ _____	Student attempts, with some success, to use new and sophisticated vocabulary to convey meaning. Comments: _____ _____ _____

Entry 2

Read the following paragraph. The underlined words are very simple, and are not very interesting. Re-write the paragraph, and change as many of the underlined words as you can – use more interesting words that say more.

Little kids are <u>good</u>. They can <u>move</u>. They can <u>talk about</u> <u>good</u> <u>things</u>. Sometimes little kids <u>do bad things</u>. Sometimes they <u>get</u> <u>dirt on themselves</u>. Still, I think that <u>little kids</u> are <u>good</u>.

_____

_____

_____

_____

_____

_____

_____

_____

_____

_____

Trait Assessment
Trait: Word Choice
Success Descriptors (Circle one and add your own comments)

Not Yet	Emerging	Effective	Strong
Does not write in English. Words are too inaccurate or badly spelled to determine meaning.

Comments: _____
_____
_____ | Words are simple and/or not the most accurate choice. Some inaccurate word choices are made.

Comments: _____
_____
_____ | Student uses familiar vocabulary to accurately convey his or her meaning.

Comments: _____
_____
_____ | Student attempts, with some success, to use new and sophisticated vocabulary to convey meaning.

Comments: _____
_____
_____ |

Entry 3

Read the following paragraph. The sentences are short, and they all sound the same. Try to re-write the paragraph and talk about the same things, but change the sentences so that they are longer, or are different from each other.

Mike is tall. Mike is smart. Mike is a fast runner. Mike is a person who plays football. Mike is a person with a girlfriend. Mike is a cool person.

_____

_____

_____

_____

_____

_____

_____

_____

_____

_____

Trait Assessment
Trait: Sentence Fluency
Success Descriptors (Circle one and add your own comments)

Not Yet	Emerging	Effective	Strong
Does not write in English. Does not write complete sentences. Does not write more than one sentence.	Two or more complete sentences are present, but there are problems with grammar or a repetitive sentence pattern.	Two or more complete sentences are present and are grammatically correct. There is variation in the sentence structures.	Two or more complete and correct sentences are present, there is variation in structure and that variation enhances the flow and readability of the piece.
Comments: _____ _____	Comments: _____ _____	Comments: _____ _____	Comments: _____ _____

Entry 4

Read the following paragraph. The sentences are short, and they all sound the same. Try to re-write the paragraph and talk about the same things, but change the sentences so that they are longer, or are different from each other.

Clouds look like white things. Clouds look like puffy balls. Clouds look like flat, gray sheets. Clouds look like rain is coming. Clouds look like pictures of things. Clouds look like smoke.

_____

_____

_____

_____

_____

_____

_____

_____

_____

Trait Assessment
Trait: Sentence Fluency
Success Descriptors (Circle one and add your own comments)

Not Yet	Emerging	Effective	Strong
Does not write in English. Does not write complete sentences. Does not write more than one sentence.	Two or more complete sentences are present, but there are problems with grammar or a repetitive sentence pattern.	Two or more complete sentences are present and are grammatically correct. There is variation in the sentence structures.	Two or more complete and correct sentences are present, there is variation in structure and that variation enhances the flow and readability of the piece.
Comments: _____ _____ _____	Comments: _____ _____ _____	Comments: _____ _____ _____	Comments: _____ _____ _____

Entry 5

Read the following poem. Notice how it is made with one word going down, and sentences talking about that word, starting with each letter of the word.

Calculate hard math problems.
Organize your addresses.
Mail jokes to your friends.
Print pictures of rock stars.
Understand more about science.
Talk to your friends on message boards.
Explode bad guys in games.
Read about the whole world.
The going-down word is "computer," and each line of the poem talks about what you can do with a computer. Try one of your own, using the word "family."

F_____

A_____

M_____

I_____

L_____

Y_____

Trait Assessment
Trait: Word Choice
Success Descriptors (Circle one and add your own comments)

Not Yet	Emerging	Effective	Strong
Does not write in English. Words are too inaccurate or badly spelled to determine meaning.

Comments: _____ _____ | Words are simple and/or not the most accurate choice. Some inaccurate word choices are made.

Comments: _____ _____ | Student uses familiar vocabulary to accurately convey his or her meaning.

Comments: _____ _____ | Student attempts, with some success, to use new and sophisticated vocabulary to convey meaning.

Comments: _____ _____ |

Entry 6

Write your own word poem, like the ones in Entry 5. Think of your own going-down word, and what you will say about that word on each line.

_____

_____

_____

_____

_____

_____

_____

_____

_____

_____

_____

_____

Trait Assessment
Trait: Organization
Success Descriptors (Circle one and add your own comments)

Not Yet	Emerging	Effective	Strong
Student does not respond to prompt, does not include elements required by prompt, and/or no thought-out order is apparent in the response. Comments: _____ _____	Sentences follow a logical order, but it is a simple order that does not reflect understanding of the need for organization specific to the prompt. Comments: _____ _____	Sentences follow an order that is logical in responding to the prompt. Comments: _____ _____	Organization is unique, creative, and enhances the meaning of the student's response. Comments: _____ _____

Entry 7

Read the following poem.

1.   I never saw a purple *cow*.
2.   I never hope to see <u>one</u>.
3.   But I can tell you here and *now*,
4.   I'd rather see than be <u>one</u>!

Notice that the words at the end of Line 1 and Line 3 have the same ending sound – "ow." Also, the words at the end of Line 2 and Line 4 end with the same sound.

Make your own version of the poem on the lines below.
Be sure that the words that end your Line 1 and Line 3 have the same ending sound, and that the words ending your Line 2 and Line 4 have the same sound.

1.   I never _____

2.   I never _____

3.   But I can tell you _____

4.   I _____

Trait Assessment
Trait: Word Choice
Success Descriptors (Circle one and add your own comments)

Not Yet	Emerging	Effective	Strong
Does not write in English. Words are too inaccurate or badly spelled to determine meaning.

Comments: _____
_____
_____ | Words are simple and/or not the most accurate choice. Some inaccurate word choices are made.

Comments: _____
_____
_____ | Student uses familiar vocabulary to accurately convey his or her meaning.

Comments: _____
_____
_____ | Student attempts, with some success, to use new and sophisticated vocabulary to convey meaning.

Comments: _____
_____
_____ |

Entry 8

Now you are going to write a whole poem with the same rhyme pattern as the one you read in Entry 7. Re-read the poem, and notice that, not only do ending words sound the same, but that each line has the same rhythm.

1.
1 2 3 4 5 6 7 8
I never saw a purple cow.

2.
1 2 3 4 5 6 7
I never hope to see one.

3.
1 2 3 4 5 6 7 8
But I can tell you here and now,

4.
1 2 3 4 5 6 7
I'd rather see than be one!

Line 1 and Line 3 each have 8 beats, or use 8 syllables. Line 2 and Line 4 each have 7 beats, or 7 syllables. **Now it's your turn.** Write a poem about anything you'd like, but make sure that Line 1 and Line 3 rhyme (have the same ending sound), and that Line 2 and Line 4 rhyme. Also try to write it so that Line 1 and Line 3 have 8 beats (syllables) and Line 2 and Line 4 have 7 beats (syllables).

1. _____

2. _____

3. _____

4. _____

Trait Assessment
Trait: Ideas
Success Descriptors (Circle one and add your own comments)

Not Yet	Emerging	Effective	Strong
Does not answer prompt.	Most ideas address the prompt, but some are off-topic.	Ideas address the prompt to the degree requested.	Ideas address the prompt and extend beyond the degree requested. Student approaches the topic from a unique point of view.
Comments: _____ _____ _____	Comments: _____ _____ _____	Comments: _____ _____ _____	Comments: _____ _____ _____

Entry 9

The following poem is a Limerick. A Limerick has five lines. Lines 1, 2, and 5 rhyme with each other. Lines 3 and 4 rhyme with each other. A Limerick also has a specific beat pattern – Lines 1 and 2 have 8 beats. Lines 3 and 4 have 6 beats, and Line 5 has 9 beats.

1.   There once was a girl from Peru,
2.   Whose favorite color was blue.
3.   She got paint and a brush,
4.   And she worked in a rush,
5.   'Till the world had been painted her hue.

Finish the lines below to make a Limerick of your own. The rhyming words are there for you, so you just have to make sure you have the right number of beats, and that your poem makes sense!

1. _____ Milan,

2. _____ pan.

3. _____ car,

4. _____ far,

5. _____ can!

Trait Assessment
Trait: Ideas
Success Descriptors (Circle one and add your own comments)

Not Yet	Emerging	Effective	Strong
Does not answer prompt.	Most ideas address the prompt, but some are off-topic.	Ideas address the prompt to the degree requested.	Ideas address the prompt and extend beyond the degree requested. Student approaches the topic from a unique point of view.
Comments: _____ _____ _____	Comments: _____ _____ _____	Comments: _____ _____ _____	Comments: _____ _____ _____

Entry 10

Now you need to write your own Limerick, with no help at all!

Remember: Line 1 – 8 beats, rhyme A
              Line 2 – 8 beats, rhyme A
              Line 3 – 6 beats, rhyme B
              Line 4 – 6 beats, rhyme B
              Line 5 – 9 beats, rhyme A

1. _____

2. _____

3. _____

4. _____

5. _____

Trait Assessment
Trait: Organization
Success Descriptors (Circle one and add your own comments)

Not Yet	Emerging	Effective	Strong
Student does not respond to prompt, does not include elements required by prompt, and/or no thought-out order is apparent in the response.	Sentences follow a logical order, but it is a simple order that does not reflect understanding of the need for organization specific to the prompt.	Sentences follow an order that is logical in responding to the prompt.	Organization is unique, creative, and enhances the meaning of the student's response.
Comments: _____ _____ _____	Comments: _____ _____ _____	Comments: _____ _____ _____	Comments: _____ _____ _____

Entry 11

What is your favorite movie? Why is it the best movie? Fill in the blanks below. Write complete sentences to explain about your favorite movie.

I think that _____

is the best movie ever.

I like it because _____

Give another reason why it is the best movie: _____

Give a third reason why this is your favorite movie: _____

Trait Assessment
Trait: Conventions
Success Descriptors (Circle one and add your own comments)

Not Yet	Emerging	Effective	Strong
Not answered in English. Incomplete sentences. Failure to produce capitalization, ending punctuation. Spelling that renders the work incomprehensible.	Complete sentences. Capitalization and ending punctuation. Spelling, grammar, and interior punctuation errors occur but do not obscure the meaning of the response.	Complete sentences, capitalization, ending punctuation all present. No grammar mistakes in terms of conjugation, plurals, or articles. Grammar mistakes beyond direct-instruction do not obscure meaning. Minimal spelling errors.	Complete and complex sentences with no errors at all.
Comments: _____ _____	Comments: _____ _____	Comments: _____ _____	Comments: _____ _____

Entry 12

Do you think that any person should be able to come live in the United States if he or she wants to? OR, do you think that there should be rules that allow some people to come to live in the United States, and rules that keep other people out?
Write your answers in complete sentences in the blanks below.

I think that _____

_____

One reason I am right is because _____

I am also right because _____

_____

A third reason I am right is because _____

_____

Trait Assessment
Trait: Ideas
Success Descriptors (Circle one and add your own comments)

Not Yet	Emerging	Effective	Strong
Does not answer prompt.	Most ideas address the prompt, but some are off-topic.	Ideas address the prompt to the degree requested.	Ideas address the prompt and extend beyond the degree requested. Student approaches the topic from a unique point of view.
Comments: _____ _____ _____	Comments: _____ _____ _____	Comments: _____ _____ _____	Comments: _____ _____ _____

Entry 13

What is a "student"? Fill in the blanks below with complete sentences to explain what the word "student" means.

A student is _____

Tell more about what the word "student" means: _____

Tell about what a "student" does: _____

How do you know a person is a "student"? _____

Trait Assessment
Trait: Conventions
Success Descriptors (Circle one and add your own comments)

Not Yet	Emerging	Effective	Strong
Not answered in English. Incomplete sentences. Failure to produce capitalization, ending punctuation. Spelling that renders the work incomprehensible.	Complete sentences. Capitalization and ending punctuation. Spelling, grammar, and interior punctuation errors occur but do not obscure the meaning of the response.	Complete sentences, capitalization, ending punctuation all present. No grammar mistakes in terms of conjugation, plurals, or articles. Grammar mistakes beyond direct-instruction do not obscure meaning. Minimal spelling errors.	Complete and complex sentences with no errors at all.
Comments: _____ _____ _____	Comments: _____ _____ _____	Comments: _____ _____ _____	Comments: _____ _____ _____

Entry 14

What does the word "law" mean? Fill in the blanks below with complete sentences to explain what the word "law" means.

A law is _____

_____

Who makes laws? _____

What are laws for? What do laws do? _____

_____

What happens when people do not obey a law? _____

_____

Trait Assessment
Trait: Ideas
Success Descriptors (Circle one and add your own comments)

Not Yet	Emerging	Effective	Strong
Does not answer prompt.	Most ideas address the prompt, but some are off-topic.	Ideas address the prompt to the degree requested.	Ideas address the prompt and extend beyond the degree requested. Student approaches the topic from a unique point of view.
Comments: _____ _____ _____	Comments: _____ _____ _____	Comments: _____ _____ _____	Comments: _____ _____ _____

Entry 15
Look at this photograph. Fill in the blanks below with complete sentences that talk about what you see in the photograph. Use complete sentences. Try to use words that will help someone who can't see the photograph understand what you see.

This is a picture of _____

_____

I can see _____

I can also see _____

_____

Another thing I see is _____

_____

Entry 15 (continued)

Trait Assessment
Trait: Ideas
Success Descriptors (Circle one and add your own comments)

Not Yet	Emerging	Effective	Strong
Does not answer prompt.	Most ideas address the prompt, but some are off-topic.	Ideas address the prompt to the degree requested.	Ideas address the prompt and extend beyond the degree requested. Student approaches the topic from a unique point of view.
Comments: _____ _____ _____	Comments: _____ _____ _____	Comments: _____ _____ _____	Comments: _____ _____ _____

Entry 16
Look at this photograph. Fill in the blanks below with complete sentences that talk about what you see in the photograph. Use complete sentences. Try to use words that will help someone who can't see the photograph understand what you see.

This is a picture of _____

_____

I can see _____

I can also see _____

_____

Another thing I see is _____

_____

Entry 16 (continued)

Trait Assessment
Trait: Conventions
Success Descriptors (Circle one and add your own comments)

Not Yet	Emerging	Effective	Strong
Not answered in English. Incomplete sentences. Failure to produce capitalization, ending punctuation. Spelling that renders the work incomprehensible.	Complete sentences. Capitalization and ending punctuation. Spelling, grammar, and interior punctuation errors occur but do not obscure the meaning of the response.	Complete sentences, capitalization, ending punctuation all present. No grammar mistakes in terms of conjugation, plurals, or articles. Grammar mistakes beyond direct-instruction do not obscure meaning. Minimal spelling errors.	Complete and complex sentences with no errors at all.
Comments: _____ _____ _____	Comments: _____ _____ _____	Comments: _____ _____ _____	Comments: _____ _____ _____

Entry 17

Imagine that you got to ride on the Space Shuttle to the Moon. Tell the story of your trip. Use your imagination and talk about all the interesting things you saw and did when you went to the moon.

_____

_____

_____

_____

_____

_____

_____

_____

_____

_____

_____

_____

_____

_____

_____

_____

Trait Assessment

Trait: Sentence Fluency

Success Descriptors (Circle one and add your own comments)

Not Yet	Emerging	Effective	Strong
Does not write in English. Does not write complete sentences. Does not write more than one sentence.	Two or more complete sentences are present, but there are problems with grammar or a repetitive sentence pattern.	Two or more complete sentences are present and are grammatically correct. There is variation in the sentence structures.	Two or more complete and correct sentences are present, there is variation in structure and that variation enhances the flow and readability of the piece.
Comments: _____ _____ _____	Comments: _____ _____ _____	Comments: _____ _____ _____	Comments: _____ _____ _____

Entry 18

Think about a home you lived in before you moved to the United States. How would you tell a person who has never seen this home what it looks like, so that they could see what you remember?

_____

_____

_____

_____

_____

_____

_____

_____

_____

_____

_____

_____

_____

_____

_____

_____

_____

_____

_____

Trait Assessment
Trait: Word Choice
Success Descriptors (Circle one and add your own comments)

Not Yet	Emerging	Effective	Strong
Does not write in English. Words are too inaccurate or badly spelled to determine meaning. Comments: _____ _____ _____	Words are simple and/or not the most accurate choice. Some inaccurate word choices are made. Comments: _____ _____ _____	Student uses familiar vocabulary to accurately convey his or her meaning. Comments: _____ _____ _____	Student attempts, with some success, to use new and sophisticated vocabulary to convey meaning. Comments: _____ _____ _____

Entry 19

What does the word "responsibility" mean? Explain what you think "responsibility" is. How do people act, if they act with responsibility? Why should people learn about responsibility?

_____

_____

_____

_____

_____

_____

_____

_____

_____

_____

_____

_____

_____

_____

_____

_____

Trait Assessment
Trait: Ideas
Success Descriptors (Circle one and add your own comments)

Not Yet	Emerging	Effective	Strong
Does not answer prompt.	Most ideas address the prompt, but some are off-topic.	Ideas address the prompt to the degree requested.	Ideas address the prompt and extend beyond the degree requested. Student approaches the topic from a unique point of view.
Comments: _____ _____ _____	Comments: _____ _____ _____	Comments: _____ _____ _____	Comments: _____ _____ _____

Entry 20

Your class is going to take a field trip to Washington D.C. You really want to go, and you think you will learn a lot there. Your parents do not want you to go, because they are worried about how much money it will cost, and they are worried that you will not be safe. Write a note to your parents that gives three reasons why they should let you go to Washington D.C.

_____

_____

_____

_____

_____

_____

_____

_____

_____

_____

_____

_____

_____

_____

_____

_____

_____

Trait Assessment
Trait: Organization
Success Descriptors (Circle one and add your own comments)

Not Yet	Emerging	Effective	Strong
Student does not respond to prompt, does not include elements required by prompt, and/or no thought-out order is apparent in the response. Comments: _____ _____ _____	Sentences follow a logical order, but it is a simple order that does not reflect understanding of the need for organization specific to the prompt. Comments: _____ _____ _____	Sentences follow an order that is logical in responding to the prompt. Comments: _____ _____ _____	Organization is unique, creative, and enhances the meaning of the student's response. Comments: _____ _____ _____

Section Four:
Paragraphs

For the teacher...

Trait: Voice

Some time ago, when folks were just using e-mail and I was away at college, my father introduced me to a game (what would, a decade later, be called a "meme" I guess) in which you wrote the punch-line of the "Why did the chicken cross the road?" joke as a famous author would write it. We'd think up authors with distinctive styles and send each other the name, challenging each other to write the joke in the author's voice. The classic example is Hemingway's response: "To die. In the rain." When explaining the trait of Voice to teachers, I often use this story, as the game was exploring Voice in its essence.

For all of its subjective vagary, Voice is an extremely important trait, and also one which an English language learner can explore with success even before he or she has developed a great deal of proficiency. If you think about your class, you know each of your students already has a unique voice, a personality that comes through what they say and what they do. The trick now is to encourage them to harness it in order to create the author-to-audience connection that is essential in good writing.

Syndicated columnist Dave Barry has a very distinctive voice. The humor in his columns derives not so much from the subject matter (which often ranges from the mundane to the moronic – I'm saying this as a fan) but in how he discusses it: often with hyperbole, all capital letters and booger jokes. Regular readers of Dave Barry could easily identify a piece of his writing, even if they've never read it before, from the voice.

To help your students learn more about voice, try contrasting authors that they have studied who have distinctive styles. After reading a piece by a certain author, present them with several excerpts, including one they haven't read by that same author, and see if they can pick out his or her work. Discuss what features helped them identify the author by voice.

Voice goes beyond imprint of personality. Voice also includes the writer's awareness of the audience and purpose of the piece. When Dave Barry was a regular reporter at the dawn of his career, he wrote straight news stories and refrained from abusing the caps lock or using the word "booger." Secondary students need direct instruction in the importance of register, or how formal or informal a piece of writing may be. When discussing this with your students, contrast formal and informal writing – a text message versus a business memo, a rap song versus a hymn, lecture notes versus a term paper – and discuss what factors of vocabulary and syntax affect the register.

Model Lesson 6 – Introducing Voice

Content Objective: Students will be able to explain the two elements of the trait of Voice.

Language Objective: Students will be able to list the two elements of the trait Voice. Students will be able to differentiate between formal register and informal register.

Building Background/Connecting With Prior Knowledge:

Ask the students to find the correct ending to each sentence in the second column:

1. What we choose to write about are our _____.

A. Organization

B. Sentence Fluency

2. Which words we choose to use is our _____.

C. Ideas

3. How we put ideas in order is our

_____ .

D. Conventions

E. Word Choice

4. Correct spelling, punctuation and capitalization are _____.

5. How varied sentences are and how well they sound when read aloud is _____ .

Tell the students that today's trait is Voice. Ask them to write down a sentence guessing what Voice has to do with writing. Share the responses. This is just to get thinking, they don't have to be right… yet.

Teacher Input:

Remind students that writing is moving an idea from your mind to someone else's mind. It's like getting a paper airplane from one person to another. Give a student on one end of the room a paper airplane. Choose a student on the other end of the room. How will the first student get the paper airplane to the student across the room? The only rule is that the second student doesn't get up. Write suggestions on the board.

If throwing the paper airplane is a suggestion, ask, what does the student need to do when he or she throws it, to make sure the other person gets it? They need to know where the student is (aim) and they need to throw hard enough – but not too hard. Note these considerations on the board as well.

Students might also suggest walking across the room with the paper airplane, or passing it from desk to desk. Again, ask them about what they need to do in order to make sure the paper airplane reaches its intended target.

Present students with the following letter:

Hey, Mr. Johnson!

What's up? Can you give me a job at your bank, man? That would be so cool! 'Cause, I love money, you know? Text me and tell me what you think!

Later,
David

What is wrong with this letter? Hopefully the students can identify that the tone is inappropriate for a request for a job. Tell them about:
formal register: how you should write or speak when addressing strangers, especially in business or school
informal register: how you write or speak when addressing your friends

So: part number 1 of Voice is:
Show in your writing that you know who your audience is. Change your writing so that it reaches them. (Write this on the board).

How is this like the problem with the paper airplane? Relate to thinking about where the person is/who the person is in relationship to you.

As a group, re-write David's letter so that it is in the appropriate register. Point out that the driving force is not who David is, but who his audience is.

There is a second part to voice, as there are two people involved with throwing the paper airplane. Show that the paper airplane used in the first exercise is plain. If the paper airplane gets to the person it's intended for, how does that person know who the paper airplane is from?

Hand out plain copier paper. Each sheet should have one student's name on it – but don't give students their own name. The name is of the person the paper airplane will be going to. Hand out markers/ crayons/ map pencils. The task is that each student will make a paper airplane and decorate it. They MAY NOT write their names anywhere on the plane, but instead must decorate it in such a way that the recipient can guess who the airplane came from.

If you need instructions on how to fold a paper airplane, go to
http://www.ehow.com/how_839_make-paper-airplane.html .

So, when the airplanes are decorated, then the students need to get the planes to person whose name is on the plane. Tell them the only rule is that they can't hand it to them directly. Once the chaos has died down, ask the students if they all got the plane with their name on it. If the answer is yes, write "100%!" on the board next to "Part number 1 of Voice is...".

Next, write on the board:
Part number 2 of Voice is: Good writing shows who the writer is.

Have each student guess where their airplane came from. If they get it all right, you can put another "100%" on the board.

Share the student-friendly rubric for voice with the students. Relate it to the two "parts" of Voice you have on the board.

Review for Mastery:
Students need to answer, orally or in writing:
- Why did you make sure the paper airplane got to the right person?
- Why did you decorate your paper airplane?
- What does your paper airplane remind you about when you are writing?

The trait descriptors for Voice are:

Trait: Voice
Success Descriptors

Not Yet	Emerging	Effective	Strong
No attempt is made to connect with the audience or address the purpose of the prompt. Writing is definitely uninspired, lifeless, mechanical.	The student attempts to engage the audience and address the purpose, but fails to make a perceivable connection. Writing may be somewhat lifeless, mechanical.	The response shows an awareness of the purpose and audience for this prompt. The student reveals their personality to some degree.	Response is engaging and appropriate to purpose and audience. The writer reveals a style that clearly reflects his or her personality.

Chapter Four Activities:

In this section, students will be given 10 writing assignments that are a little more expansive than in previous sections. Each prompt will have a planning page, then a final assignment page. To move students toward a time when their work will be evaluated on all seven traits at once, each entry will be evaluated on two of the traits. Several tasks are designed to directly address Voice and will have Voice as one of those traits.

Remember, as you evaluate for any trait, that, while the tasks are more extensive, you should have a clear understanding at this point for what each student is ready to do. Some students may be comfortable or adventurous enough with their English to employ varied sentence patterns and advanced vocabulary and others may not. Yet all should be able to complete the assigned task with your guidance and the guidance of the planning page to the best of their abilities. On the next page all of the traits are again presented in student-friendly language.

Student-Friendly Rubric

TRAIT	Not Yet	Emerging	Effective	Strong
Ideas	Does not answer prompt.	Most ideas address the prompt, but some are off-topic.	Ideas address the prompt to the degree requested.	Ideas address the prompt and extend beyond the degree requested. Student approaches the topic from a unique point of view.
Organization	Student does not respond to prompt, does not include elements required by prompt, and/or no thought-out order is apparent in the response.	Sentences follow a logical order, but it is a simple order that does not reflect understanding of the need for organization specific to the prompt.	Sentences follow an order that is logical in responding to the prompt.	Organization is unique, creative, and enhances the meaning of the student's response.
Word Choice	Does not write in English. Words are too inaccurate or badly spelled to determine meaning.	Words are simple and/or not the most accurate choice. Some inaccurate word choices are made.	Student uses familiar vocabulary to accurately convey his or her meaning.	Student attempts, with some success, to use new and sophisticated vocabulary to convey meaning.
Sentence Fluency	Does not write in English. Does not write complete sentences. Does not write more than one sentence.	Two or more complete sentences are present, but there is a repetitive sentence pattern.	Two or more complete sentences are present and are grammatically correct. There is variation in the sentence structures.	Two or more complete and correct sentences are present, there is variation in structure and that variation enhances the flow and readability of the piece.
Voice	No attempt is made to connect with the audience or address the purpose of the prompt. Writing is definitely uninspired, lifeless, mechanical.	The student attempts to engage the audience and address the purpose, but fails to make a perceivable connection. Writing may be somewhat lifeless, mechanical.	The response shows an awareness of the purpose and audience for this prompt. The student reveals their personality to some degree.	Response is engaging and appropriate to purpose and audience. The writer reveals a style that clearly reflects his or her personality.
Conventions	Not answered in English. Incomplete sentences. Failure to produce capitalization, ending punctuation. Spelling that renders the work incomprehensible.	Complete sentences. Capitalization and ending punctuation. Spelling, grammar, and interior punctuation errors occur but do not obscure the meaning of the response.	Complete sentences, capitalization, ending punctuation all present. No grammar mistakes in areas that have been directly taught. Grammar mistakes beyond direct-instruction do not obscure meaning. Minimal spelling errors.	Complete and complex sentences with no errors at all.

Entry 1
Why We Came to America

Write a speech which you would say to students at school who do not come from another country. Explain why your family chose to leave your home country and come to the United States.

Fill out the following to help you plan what you will say in your speech:

Things I/my family love about my home country:

_____

_____

_____

_____

Things I/my family found difficult in my home country:	**How coming to the United States could help:**
_____	_____
_____	_____
_____	_____
_____	_____
_____	_____
_____	_____

What else should students know about your family's choice to move to the United States?

_____

_____

_____

_____

Entry 1
Why We Came to America

Write a speech which you would say to students at school who do not come from another country. Explain why your family chose to leave your home country and come to the United States. Use the ideas you wrote down on the planning page.

_____
_____
_____
_____
_____
_____
_____
_____
_____
_____
_____
_____
_____
_____
_____
_____
_____
_____
_____
_____
_____
_____
_____
_____
_____
_____
_____

Entry 1 (continued)

Trait Assessment
Trait: Ideas
Success Descriptors (Circle one and add your own comments)

Not Yet	Emerging	Effective	Strong
Does not answer prompt.	Most ideas address the prompt, but some are off-topic.	Ideas address the prompt to the degree requested.	Ideas address the prompt and extend beyond the degree requested. Student approaches the topic from a unique point of view.
Comments: _____ _____ _____	Comments: _____ _____ _____	Comments: _____ _____ _____	Comments: _____ _____ _____

Trait Assessment
Trait: Conventions
Success Descriptors (Circle one and add your own comments)

Not Yet	Emerging	Effective	Strong
Not answered in English. Incomplete sentences. Failure to produce capitalization, ending punctuation. Spelling that renders the work incomprehensible.	Complete sentences. Capitalization and ending punctuation. Spelling, grammar, and interior punctuation errors occur but do not obscure the meaning of the response.	Complete sentences, capitalization, ending punctuation all present. No grammar mistakes in terms of conjugation, plurals, or articles. Grammar mistakes beyond direct-instruction do not obscure meaning. Minimal spelling errors.	Complete and complex sentences with no errors at all.
Comments: _____ _____ _____	Comments: _____ _____ _____	Comments: _____ _____ _____	Comments: _____ _____ _____

Entry 2
The Dream Job

What would be the best job to have when you grow up? Learn what you would need to do to get that job, and then write a set of instructions to yourself, telling yourself how to get your dream job.

What is your dream job? _____

Talk to an adult or look up the job on the internet, so that you can answer the following questions?
What education do you need to get this job?
      high school diploma   2-year (associate's) college degree
    4-year (bachelor's) college degree   master's degree   doctorate
          certification   apprenticeship

What subjects do you need to be good at in order to do this job well?
      English   math   science   social studies
     foreign language   music   art   athletics
        electronics/computers   construction
          other _____

What special skills that are not part of school would you need? _____
_____

Some jobs, such as teacher, lawyer, or nurse, can be found as soon as you have completed the necessary education and certification. Other jobs, such at bank president, sales manager, or television producer, require that you start at a less-important job, then work hard and earn more difficult and important jobs in the industry. A third kind of job – movie star, comic book author, or pro basketball player – takes both talent and good luck.
Which one of these groups does your dream job fit into? _____
_____

Entry 2
The Dream Job

What would be the best job to have when you grow up? Learn what you would need to do to get that job, then write a set of instructions to yourself, telling yourself how to get your dream job. Look back at what you learned about your job and wrote down on your planning page, then make sure each fact is included in your set of instructions.

_____
_____
_____
_____
_____
_____
_____
_____
_____
_____
_____
_____
_____
_____
_____
_____
_____
_____
_____
_____
_____
_____
_____
_____

Entry 2 (continued)

Trait Assessment
Trait: Sentence Fluency
Success Descriptors (Circle one and add your own comments)

Not Yet	Emerging	Effective	Strong
Does not write in English. Does not write complete sentences. Does not write more than one sentence. Comments: _____ _____ _____	Two or more complete sentences are present, but there are problems with grammar or a repetitive sentence pattern. Comments: _____ _____ _____	Two or more complete sentences are present and are grammatically correct. There is variation in the sentence structures. Comments: _____ _____ _____	Two or more complete and correct sentences are present, there is variation in structure and that variation enhances the flow and readability of the piece. Comments: _____ _____ _____

Trait Assessment
Trait: Organization
Success Descriptors (Circle one and add your own comments)

Not Yet	Emerging	Effective	Strong
Student does not respond to prompt, does not include elements required by prompt, and/or no thought-out order is apparent in the response. Comments: _____ _____ _____	Sentences follow a logical order, but it is a simple order that does not reflect understanding of the need for organization specific to the prompt. Comments: _____ _____ _____	Sentences follow an order that is logical in responding to the prompt. Comments: _____ _____ _____	Organization is unique, creative, and enhances the meaning of the student's response. Comments: _____ _____ _____

Entry 3
Country Kid or City Kid?

Imagine that you live in the city, with hundreds of people all around you. You can walk to the store or the movie theater. It's loud and a little dirty, but there is always something to do. But your parents are deciding to move, and that they are planning to move to a farm out in the country. Your new house would have lots of animals, and you would be able to see fields and rivers and trees. However, you would have to drive a long way just to see another house or get to a store.

Do you like this idea or not? Write a note to your parents and tell them how you feel. If you like the idea of moving to a farm in the country, tell them why you like it. If you think moving to the country is a bad idea, explain to them why you do not like it.

Use form below to help organize your ideas.

Living in the City
Good   Bad

_____   _____
_____   _____
_____   _____
_____   _____
_____   _____
_____   _____
_____   _____
_____   _____
_____   _____

Living in the Country
Good   Bad

_____   _____
_____   _____
_____   _____
_____   _____
_____   _____
_____   _____
_____   _____
_____   _____
_____   _____

Entry 3
Country Kid or City Kid?

Imagine that you live in the city, with hundreds of people all around you. You can walk to the store or the movie theater. It's loud and a little dirty, but there is always something to do. But your parents are deciding to move, and that they are planning to move to a farm out in the country. Your new house would have lots of animals, and you would be able to see fields and rivers and trees. However, you would have to drive a long way just to see another house or get to a store.

Do you like this idea or not? Write a note to your parents and tell them how you feel. If you like the idea of moving to a farm in the country, tell them why you like it. If you think moving to the country is a bad idea, explain to them why you do not like it.

Entry 3 (continued)

Trait Assessment
Trait: Ideas
Success Descriptors (Circle one and add your own comments)

Not Yet	Emerging	Effective	Strong
Does not answer prompt.	Most ideas address the prompt, but some are off-topic.	Ideas address the prompt to the degree requested.	Ideas address the prompt and extend beyond the degree requested. Student approaches the topic from a unique point of view.
Comments: _____ _____ _____	Comments: _____ _____ _____	Comments: _____ _____ _____	Comments: _____ _____ _____

Trait: Word Choice
Success Descriptors (Circle one and add your own comments)

Not Yet	Emerging	Effective	Strong
Does not write in English. Words are too inaccurate or badly spelled to determine meaning.	Words are simple and/or not the most accurate choice. Some inaccurate word choices are made.	Student uses familiar vocabulary to accurately convey his or her meaning.	Student attempts, with some success, to use new and sophisticated vocabulary to convey meaning.
Comments: _____ _____ _____	Comments: _____ _____ _____	Comments: _____ _____ _____	Comments: _____ _____ _____

Entry 4
In the News

Look! You've just made the front page of the newspaper! Write the headline and the news story about what you did.

Newspaper reporters must always include "who, what, where, why and when" in their stories. This means they must say *who* were the people in the story, *what* they did, *where* they did it, *why* they did it and *when* they did it. Think about your news story then fill out the form:

Who: _____

_____

What: _____

_____

Where: _____

_____

Why: _____

_____

When: _____

_____

Newspaper headlines are short and try to be interesting or exciting. They are not usually complete sentences. Here are some example headlines:

Photo Leads to Changes at Charter School*
Blast on Moscow Subway Kills 37
Rally Protests Illegal Immigration Deportation Law

Look at your local newspaper and find some more headlines. How do they tell you about the story, and how do they make people interested in the story? Think about your story and write a few practice headlines below:

_____

_____

_____

_____

_____

_____

* headlines from March 29, 2010 *Charlotte Observer* at www.charlotteobserver.com

Entry 4
In the News

Look! You've just made the front page of the newspaper! Write the headline and the news story about what you did. Will one of your practice headlines from the planning page work? Make sure to include all of the who-what-where-why-when facts you wrote on your planning page in your story.

_____

(Headline)

_____
_____
_____
_____
_____
_____
_____
_____
_____
_____
_____
_____
_____
_____
_____
_____
_____
_____
_____
_____
_____

Entry 4 (continued)

Trait Assessment
Trait: Organization
Success Descriptors (Circle one and add your own comments)

Not Yet	Emerging	Effective	Strong
Student does not respond to prompt, does not include elements required by prompt, and/or no thought-out order is apparent in the response. Comments: _____ _____ _____	Sentences follow a logical order, but it is a simple order that does not reflect understanding of the need for organization specific to the prompt. Comments: _____ _____ _____	Sentences follow an order that is logical in responding to the prompt. Comments: _____ _____ _____	Organization is unique, creative, and enhances the meaning of the student's response. Comments: _____ _____ _____

Trait: Sentence Fluency
Success Descriptors (Circle one and add your own comments)

Not Yet	Emerging	Effective	Strong
Does not write in English. Does not write complete sentences. Does not write more than one sentence. Comments: _____ _____ _____	Two or more complete sentences are present, but there are problems with grammar or a repetitive sentence pattern. Comments: _____ _____ _____	Two or more complete sentences are present and are grammatically correct. There is variation in the sentence structures. Comments: _____ _____ _____	Two or more complete and correct sentences are present, there is variation in structure and that variation enhances the flow and readability of the piece. Comments: _____ _____ _____

Entry 5
Isn't it Ironic?

The word *irony* describes a moment in a story or real life that seems to be the opposite of what you expect. For example, Amanda loves dogs, so it is *ironic* that she is allergic to them and can't keep one as a pet. Or, Brian hates dogs, so it is *ironic* that he has a job as a dog walker. Some jokes and funny stories use irony, making us laugh at the contrast between two things. Some authors use irony in their stories to make them surprising. In the movie *Avatar*, the fact that the human hero chooses to fight alongside the aliens against the other humans is a form of irony.

Think of an ironic moment or event in your life. It can be a funny or surprising story. Imagine that you are sitting next to a nice stranger on a long, boring bus ride. Tell them your ironic story.

Brainstorming:
Think of at least three different ironic events or moments you could tell about:

_____
_____

_____
_____

_____
_____

Organizing:
Remember, you are telling this story to someone who doesn't know you. Choose the best story from above, then plan out what important information is needed for the story to make sense:
Where and when does the story happen? _____
_____

Who is in the story? _____

What important facts about the people or places in the story do you need to know to understand the story? _____
_____

What happens? _____
_____

Why is it ironic? _____
_____
_____

Entry 5
Isn't it Ironic?

Think of an ironic moment or event in your life. It can be a funny or surprising story. Imagine that you are sitting next to a nice stranger on a long, boring bus ride. Tell them your ironic story. Be sure to use what you wrote on the planning page to help you.

_____
_____
_____
_____
_____
_____
_____
_____
_____
_____
_____
_____
_____
_____
_____
_____
_____
_____
_____
_____
_____
_____
_____
_____
_____
_____
_____

Entry 5 (continued)

Trait Assessment
Trait: Ideas
Success Descriptors (Circle one and add your own comments)

Not Yet	Emerging	Effective	Strong
Does not answer prompt.	Most ideas address the prompt, but some are off-topic.	Ideas address the prompt to the degree requested.	Ideas address the prompt and extend beyond the degree requested. Student approaches the topic from a unique point of view.
Comments: _____ _____ _____	Comments: _____ _____ _____	Comments: _____ _____ _____	Comments: _____ _____ _____

Trait: Sentence Fluency
Success Descriptors (Circle one and add your own comments)

Not Yet	Emerging	Effective	Strong
Does not write in English. Does not write complete sentences. Does not write more than one sentence.	Two or more complete sentences are present, but there are problems with grammar or a repetitive sentence pattern.	Two or more complete sentences are present and are grammatically correct. There is variation in the sentence structures.	Two or more complete and correct sentences are present, there is variation in structure and that variation enhances the flow and readability of the piece.
Comments: _____ _____ _____	Comments: _____ _____ _____	Comments: _____ _____ _____	Comments: _____ _____ ____

Entry 6
Pretty Ugly

Ugly things can be just as interesting (or more) than pretty things. Think of an especially ugly place or thing (not a person, let's be nice) that you have seen, then describe it in an e-mail to a friend who lives far away from you and would never have seen this place or thing. Make sure you give lots of details to help create a picture of how ugly this place or thing is.

Use the map below to help plan out your ideas.

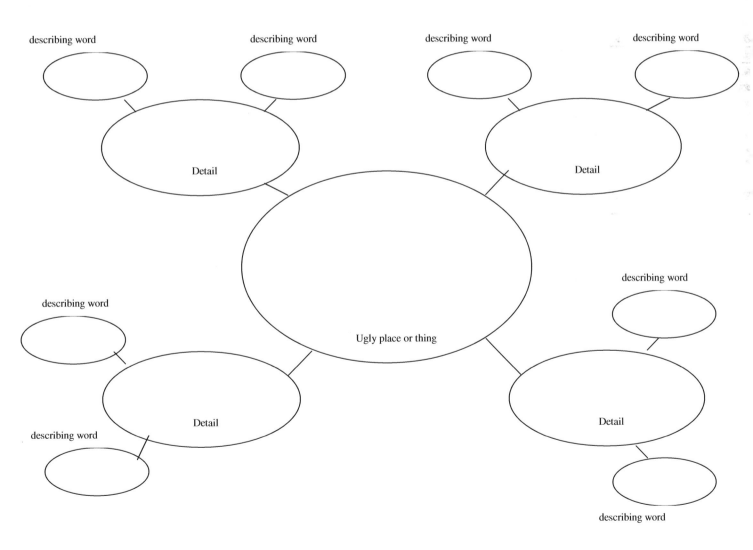

Entry 6
Pretty Ugly

Ugly things can be just as interesting (or more) than pretty things. Think of an especially ugly place or thing (not a person, let's be nice) that you have seen, then describe it in an e-mail to a friend who lives far away from you and would never have seen this place or thing. Make sure you give lots of details to help create a picture of how ugly this place or thing is. Use your ideas from the planning page to help.

_____

_____

_____

_____

_____

_____

_____

_____

_____

_____

_____

_____

_____

_____

_____

_____

_____

_____

_____

_____

_____

_____

_____

_____

Entry 6 (continued)

Trait Assessment
Trait: Word Choice
Success Descriptors (Circle one and add your own comments)

Not Yet	Emerging	Effective	Strong
Does not write in English. Words are too inaccurate or badly spelled to determine meaning. Comments: _____ _____ _____	Words are simple and/or not the most accurate choice. Some inaccurate word choices are made. Comments: _____ _____ _____	Student uses familiar vocabulary to accurately convey his or her meaning. Comments: _____ _____ _____	Student attempts, with some success, to use new and sophisticated vocabulary to convey meaning. Comments: _____ _____ _____

Trait: Sentence Fluency
Success Descriptors (Circle one and add your own comments)

Not Yet	Emerging	Effective	Strong
Does not write in English. Does not write complete sentences. Does not write more than one sentence. Comments: _____ _____ _____	Two or more complete sentences are present, but there are problems with grammar or a repetitive sentence pattern. Comments: _____ _____ _____	Two or more complete sentences are present and are grammatically correct. There is variation in the sentence structures. Comments: _____ _____ _____	Two or more complete and correct sentences are present, there is variation in structure and that variation enhances the flow and readability of the piece. Comments: _____ _____ _____

Entry 7
Letter of Recommendation

When you apply for college or for a job, you often will be asked for *references* or *letters of recommendation*. This means the college or company wants to learn more about you from someone who knows you. You will probably ask a teacher, a boss you've already had, a friend, or an adult you know in your community to be your *reference* and write your *letter of recommendation*. Perhaps one of your friends will ask you to write a letter of recommendation for them. Think of a classmate that you admire, and imagine that he or she has asked you to write a letter of recommendation for them to include in their college application. Letters of recommendation are very formal, so use the format below to help plan your letter.

Formal letters always begin with the full address of whomever you are writing to:
Admissions Department
Goode State University
100 University Place, Suite 16
Collegetown, NC 28123

If you don't know the name of the person you are writing to, the following is appropriate:
Dear Sir or Madam:

This is often how letters of recommendation begin. Fill in the blanks with the correct information.
I am writing to recommend _____ for acceptance
                              (name of friend)
into Goode State University. I have known _____
                                          (name of friend)
through _____ for _____ years, and I
  (how do you know them? school? church? work?)   (how long?)
believe that (he/she) would be a good addition to your school.

Now, think of several reasons why you admire this person. Remember, you're trying to impress an adult officer of a university about a future student, so some facts are more useful than others.
Reason 1: _____
_____
_____

Reason 2: _____
_____
_____

Reason 3: _____
_____
_____

The endings of formal letters of recommendation follow a pattern as well. Fill in the blanks with the correct information.
As you can see, _____ has many good qualities that would
                (name of friend)
make them an excellent student at Goode State University. If you have
any further questions that I can answer, please feel free to contact me.
My information is given below. Thank you for your time.

Sincerely,
_____   -- your signature
_____   -- your name
_____   -- your street address
_____   -- your city, state and zip code
_____   -- your phone number
_____   -- your e-mail address

Entry 7
Letter of Recommendation

Think of a classmate that you admire, and imagine that he or she has asked you to write a letter of recommendation for them to include in their college application. Letters of recommendation are very formal, so follow the format on the planning page to write your letter.

Entry 7 (continued)

Trait Assessment
Trait: Conventions
Success Descriptors (Circle one and add your own comments)

Not Yet	Emerging	Effective	Strong
Not answered in English. Incomplete sentences. Failure to produce capitalization, ending punctuation. Spelling that renders the work incomprehensible.	Complete sentences. Capitalization and ending punctuation. Spelling, grammar, and interior punctuation errors occur but do not obscure the meaning of the response.	Complete sentences, capitalization, ending punctuation all present. No grammar mistakes in terms of conjugation, plurals, or articles. Grammar mistakes beyond direct-instruction do not obscure meaning. Minimal spelling errors.	Complete and complex sentences with no errors at all.
Comments: _____ _____ _____	Comments: _____ _____ _____	Comments: _____ _____ _____	Comments: _____ _____ _____

Trait: Voice
Success Descriptors

Not Yet	Emerging	Effective	Strong
No attempt is made to connect with the audience or address the purpose of the prompt. Writing is definitely uninspired, lifeless, mechanical.	The student attempts to engage the audience and address the purpose, but fails to make a perceivable. connection. Writing may be somewhat lifeless, mechanical.	The response shows an awareness of the purpose and audience for this prompt. The student reveals their personality to some degree.	Response is engaging and appropriate to purpose and audience. The writer reveals a style that clearly reflects his or her personality.

Entry 8
Why the Sky is Blue

A five year old child has asked you why the sky is blue. There are two ways you can handle this: explain, in words a small child can understand, the science behind why the sky is blue, or make up a funny story that a child would like to explain why the sky is blue. Have fun either way, just remember that your audience is five years old.

If you're having trouble deciding which way to answer, use the planning page to brainstorm ideas for either response, then see where you came up with more or better ideas.

The Scientific Explanation for Why the Sky is Blue:

_____
_____
_____
_____
_____
_____
_____
_____
_____
_____
_____
_____

A Good Story About Why the Sky is Blue:

_____
_____
_____
_____
_____
_____
_____
_____
_____
_____
_____
_____

Entry 8
Why the Sky is Blue

A five year old child has asked you why the sky is blue. There are two ways you can handle this: explain, in terms a small child can understand, the science behind why the sky is blue, or make up a funny story that a child would like to explain why the sky is blue. Have fun either way, just remember that your audience is five years old.

_____
_____
_____
_____
_____
_____
_____
_____
_____
_____
_____
_____
_____
_____
_____
_____
_____
_____
_____
_____
_____
_____
_____
_____
_____

Entry 8 (continued)

Trait Assessment
Trait: Organization
Success Descriptors (Circle one and add your own comments)

Not Yet	Emerging	Effective	Strong
Student does not respond to prompt, does not include elements required by prompt, and/or no thought-out order is apparent in the response. Comments: _____ _____ _____	Sentences follow a logical order, but it is a simple order that does not reflect understanding of the need for organization specific to the prompt. Comments: _____ _____ _____	Sentences follow an order that is logical in responding to the prompt. Comments: _____ _____ _____	Organization is unique, creative, and enhances the meaning of the student's response. Comments: _____ _____ _____

Trait: Voice
Success Descriptors

Not Yet	Emerging	Effective	Strong
No attempt is made to connect with the audience or address the purpose of the prompt. Writing is definitely uninspired, lifeless, mechanical.	The student attempts to engage the audience and address the purpose, but fails to make a perceivable. connection. Writing may be somewhat lifeless, mechanical.	The response shows an awareness of the purpose and audience for this prompt. The student reveals their personality to some degree.	Response is engaging and appropriate to purpose and audience. The writer reveals a style that clearly reflects his or her personality.

Entry 9
No Fair

Sometimes things in life are just not fair. What injustice (thing that is unfair) in the world really bothers you? Artists often use songs, poems or raps to make others aware of things they feel are important problems. Write your own song, poem or rap to make people aware of something that is unfair.

Write down the important facts about your problem here, so that you can concentrate on the musical aspect of your song/poem/rap, but not forget the important things you want people to know.

What is the problem?
_____
_____

Who does it affect?
_____
_____

Who causes the problem?
_____
_____

Why is it a problem?
_____
_____

Why is it unfair?
_____
_____

Do you have a way to fix the problem?
_____
_____

Entry 9
No Fair

Sometimes things in life are just not fair. What injustice (thing that is unfair) in the world really bothers you? Artists often use songs, poems or raps to make others aware of things they feel are important problems. Write your own song, poem or rap to make people aware of something that is unfair.

_____
_____
_____
_____
_____
_____
_____
_____
_____
_____
_____
_____
_____
_____
_____
_____
_____
_____
_____
_____
_____
_____
_____
_____

Entry 9 (continued)

Trait Assessment
Trait: Word Choice
Success Descriptors (Circle one and add your own comments)

Not Yet	Emerging	Effective	Strong
Does not write in English. Words are too inaccurate or badly spelled to determine meaning. Comments: _____ _____ _____	Words are simple and/or not the most accurate choice. Some inaccurate word choices are made. Comments: _____ _____ _____	Student uses familiar vocabulary to accurately convey his or her meaning. Comments: _____ _____ _____	Student attempts, with some success, to use new and sophisticated vocabulary to convey meaning. Comments: _____ _____ _____

Trait: Voice
Success Descriptors

Not Yet	Emerging	Effective	Strong
No attempt is made to connect with the audience or address the purpose of the prompt. Writing is definitely uninspired, lifeless, mechanical.	The student attempts to engage the audience and address the purpose, but fails to make a perceivable. connection. Writing may be somewhat lifeless, mechanical.	The response shows an awareness of the purpose and audience for this prompt. The student reveals their personality to some degree.	Response is engaging and appropriate to purpose and audience. The writer reveals a style that clearly reflects his or her personality.

Entry 10
Valedictory

When a high school class attends the graduation, one student, usually the one with the best grades, is chosen to give a *valedictory speech*. This person is called the *valedictorian*. The *valedictory speech*, said after all the graduates have been handed their diplomas, is often about good memories of high school and helpful advice or hopeful inspiration about the future and becoming an adult.

Imagine that you are the valedictorian (there's no reason why not!). What would you say in your valedictory speech at graduation? Remember that -- while the speech is delivered to your classmates -- your family, your friends' families, and your teachers are all there to honor your class on a very important occasion.

Use this space to help thing of what you should include in your speech.

Important high school memories:

_____
_____
_____
_____
_____

Helpful advice for the future:

_____
_____
_____
_____
_____

Hopeful inspiration about the future:

_____
_____
_____
_____
_____

Entry 10
Valedictory

Imagine that you are the valedictorian (there's no reason why not!). What would you say in your valedictory speech at graduation? Remember that -- while the speech is delivered to your classmates -- your family, your friends' families, and your teachers are all there to honor your class on a very important occasion.

Entry 10 (continued)

Trait Assessment
Trait: Conventions
Success Descriptors (Circle one and add your own comments)

Not Yet	Emerging	Effective	Strong
Not answered in English. Incomplete sentences. Failure to produce capitalization, ending punctuation. Spelling that renders the work incomprehensible.	Complete sentences. Capitalization and ending punctuation. Spelling, grammar, and interior punctuation errors occur but do not obscure the meaning of the response.	Complete sentences, capitalization, ending punctuation all present. No grammar mistakes in terms of conjugation, plurals, or articles. Grammar mistakes beyond direct-instruction do not obscure meaning. Minimal spelling errors.	Complete and complex sentences with no errors at all.
Comments: _____ _____ _____	Comments: _____ _____ _____	Comments: _____ _____ _____	Comments: _____ _____ _____

Trait: Voice
Success Descriptors

Not Yet	Emerging	Effective	Strong
No attempt is made to connect with the audience or address the purpose of the prompt. Writing is definitely uninspired, lifeless, mechanical.	The student attempts to engage the audience and address the purpose, but fails to make a perceivable. connection. Writing may be somewhat lifeless, mechanical.	The response shows an awareness of the purpose and audience for this prompt. The student reveals their personality to some degree.	Response is engaging and appropriate to purpose and audience. The writer reveals a style that clearly reflects his or her personality.

Made in the USA
San Bernardino, CA
06 January 2019